The Three Principles
of Outstanding Golf

How A Golfer's Mind Really Works.

by Sam Jarman

Table of Contents

Acknowledgements

There are a number of people without whom you would not be reading these words.

Jamie Smart and Garret Kramer, who between them opened my eyes to a new way of seeing the world, and a new way of playing the game I had fallen in and out of love with over the past thirty years.

Elsie Spittle, for her recollections of her friendship with Syd Banks, and her kind words of encouragement.

Alistair Tait, who edited the book, tightened and brightened my paragraphs, activated my passive sentences and specified my non specific pronouns.

Julia Jarman, a far better writer than I will ever be. Her love of books and the written word was a constant theme throughout my childhood, and was clearly more of an inspiration than I realised at the time.

My girlfriend Fenella, for her love and support, proof reading skills and the very welcome supply of coffee and the occasional beer.

Mike Snapes, Andy Pollock, Adam Jerreat, Gerry Kennedy and numerous others who offered comments, feedback and encouragement during the writing process.

David Cowap for his help with the cover design and typesetting.

My friends, lesson clients and fellow golfers at Woburn and elsewhere, for your friendship, feedback, support and companionship on and off the golf course. I have learnt at least as much from you as you have from me. Hopefully it has made us all better golfers, and will continue to do so.

Lastly to Sydney Banks, who saw what he saw, and wasn't afraid to tell the world about it.

Foreword

"It is rare these days that I come across a golf coaching book which holds my attention from start to finish. It is also rare to find a book about the mind written by someone who is genuinely at the 'coal face' of both playing and coaching as opposed to classroom theory. Sam has written such a book.

It will do what a great book should by challenging your existing beliefs and making you think about the way you either play or coach the game. It is not more of the same 'positive thinking' and 'affirmation' nonsense but a genuine inquiry about how our mind actually interacts with our body to either make or break our performance. Your game and your life can't help but be enhanced by reading this book."

Dr Karl Morris

'If the only thing people learned was not to be afraid of their experience, that alone would change the world.'

Syd Banks

CHAPTER 1

We Don't Do 'Head Stuff'.

'Golf is deceptively simple and endlessly complicated; it satisfies the soul and frustrates the intellect. It is at the same time rewarding and maddening – and without a doubt the greatest game mankind has ever invented.'

—*Arnold Palmer*

IT WAS THE SUNDAY AFTERNOON of the 2011 Players Championship at TPC Sawgrass in Florida. Cheers rang out as KJ Choi and David Toms battled for the title over the closing holes. Things were a little quieter on the front nine, and a lot less dramatic. Bad weather on Saturday meant the third round had been completed on Sunday morning. The Tour implemented a two tee start to finish the final round on schedule on Sunday evening. Players further down the field were on the golf course at the same time as the leaders.

I was watching Ian Poulter. I knew Ian from playing mini tour events years ago, and through his attachment to Woburn Golf Club. Also walking with the three ball were his wife Katie, IJP Design colleague Russell Hurd and fellow Woburn members Gary Johnstone and Steve Jensen.

Playing the back nine first, he was hitting the ball nicely but not holing anything. Very relaxed, he was chatting with his caddy Terry Mundy and exchanging some banter with Russell. We watched him hit his tee shot down the 1st. Gary, Steve and I waited to see Bubba Watson drive off in the group behind before walking across to the 2nd green to meet Ian's group as they came down the par five.

Things didn't go well. The hole is reachable in two shots and a definite birdie opportunity. Ian blocked his drive right into the trees. He found his ball, but hit a tree with his recovery shot and had to take a penalty drop. He hacked it out and laid up sixty yards short of the green. In typical, never give up Poulter fashion, he pitched to six inches for a double bogey seven.

Looking a bit disenchanted with life, he tapped in, then wandered to the back of the green and sat down in an empty marshall's seat while his two playing partners putted out. I watched from about twenty yards away as he pulled the yardage book out of his back pocket and started scribbling, intent on getting something important down on paper. Always curious about what top players are thinking, I wondered what he was writing.

The double bogey had little effect on him. He made one of the best up and downs I have ever seen on the next hole to save par.

A few weeks later, I was back at Woburn watching the English Amateur Championship being played over the Marquess course. A couple of players I worked with were competing, so I spent the morning wandering in the sunshine watching them play. As I walked back to the clubhouse, I spotted two familiar figures on the practice ground alongside the eighteenth fairway. I made my way over to find Ian and caddy Terry in animated discussion about how to use a new video camera.

'Alright if I watch you hit a few?' I asked, after we had exchanged pleasantries.

'You're fine mate', Ian replied.

I stretched out on the grass as he fired six irons onto one of the tiny practice greens halfway down the range.

After an hour it became clear he was winding down. The conversation with Terry moved on from business (his golf swing) to football, cars, recent tournaments, typical golfer chit chat. I waited for a lull in the conversation, took a deep breath, then dived in.

'Ian, I'm not sure I should ask, but do you remember the second hole at Sawgrass on Sunday? You hit it into the trees off the tee but couldn't get it back on the fairway. Then you laid it up and pitched it stiff from about sixty yards. I think you made a double?'

He looked at me quizzically for a couple of seconds. 'Err, vaguely. Why?'

'You sat down at the back of the green and wrote stuff in your yardage book for about five minutes. It looked pretty important at the time. Can I ask you what you were doing?'

'Probably just writing down my yardages and doing the scorecard.'

'So you weren't making notes or anything?'

'Notes? What about?'

3

'Well, you'd just made a mistake, and seemed a bit annoyed about it. I wondered if you were writing some notes. You know, positive mental reminders, key swing thoughts, some affirmations maybe…you know, 'Head Stuff'?

He smiled at Terry and then at me.

'No Mate… We don't do Head Stuff.'

*   *   *

Why Ian Poulter Is Better Than Me.

'Golf is a game played on a five inch course. The distance between your ears.'

—Bobby Jones

From the day I met him as a precocious eighteen year old, I've been impressed by the way Ian gets the maximum out of his game. He's a very good ball striker, but by his own admission, not the best in the world. If you didn't know and saw him on the practice range at a Tour event, you probably wouldn't pick him as a Ryder Cup legend. He's not a short hitter, but he doesn't overpower golf courses like Rory McIlroy, Dustin Johnson or Bubba Watson can.

His Ryder Cup record is phenomenal. He always seems to play his best golf when the pressure is at its highest, typified by an amazing run of birdies on the Saturday at Medinah in 2010. So why is he so good? How does he deliver so consistently in demanding situations?

Looking at the statistics, he does the simple things very well. He drives the ball in the fairway. He is excellent with his wedges. He has a great short game, and putts well, especially from inside ten feet. The short game and putting are the simplest shots in terms of technique, and you don't need to be a great athlete to be a great putter.

What you do need, are calmness, clarity of mind and imagination. Ian has these in abundance. He knows his game very well and plays to his strengths. Famously, he doesn't get nervous. When asked why, he replied,

'I'm playing the shot, not the situation.'

This statement gives an insight into why he excels when the pressure is at its most intense. I'll explain later in the book.

His passion for the game is obvious and he works hard to be the best he can be. He's very independent. He doesn't have a regular coach. He keeps things simple. As you will be aware if you follow him on Twitter, he doesn't seem care about other people's thoughts or opinions. He has a great sense of perspective. His family is by far the most important thing in his life. A bad day on the golf course is just a bad day on the golf course. Terry Mundy his long time caddy is similarly down to earth.

From talking to Ian occasionally, from conversations with his father Terry and his former coach Lee Scarbrow, I would suggest the main reason Ian plays to and beyond his potential so often is because he doesn't think too much. He trusts himself and his golf swing. He sees the shot and lets it go without worrying about the consequences.

An interviewer once asked him if he used a sports psychologist.

'Why would I want to pay someone to tell me how good I already know I am?' was his reply.

From the guy trying to break a hundred for the first time, to the tour pro trying to win his first major, most golfers agree that golf is a mental game. The importance of the mind in golf has become well recognised. Acknowledgement of its significance is increasing all the time, as is the prominence of mind coaches and sports psychologists such as Tim Gallwey, Bob Rotella, Karl Morris and Steve Peters.

Golf is a hard sport to play at a high level, week in, week out, hence the time and effort the best players spend 'working' on the mental side of their performance. Since Tiger Woods won the 2008 US Open, the last in his era of dominance, first timers won seventeen out of the next twenty majors. The world number one spot keeps changing hands. Players at the top of their game who seemed poised to dominate have dropped back into the pack.

I would suggest a golfer's mind is the greatest separator between success and failure, between champion and also-ran. More so than swing technique, physical fitness or equipment. It's perfectly possible to win important tournaments with a golf swing that doesn't fit the technical ideals promoted by commentators and golf instructors, as Graeme McDowell, Jim Furyk, Jeev Milkha Singh, Colin Montgomerie and Jordan Spieth have shown.

Camillo Villegas and Dustin Johnson are generally accepted as two of the fittest, most athletic players in the professional game. At the time of writing, neither is a major champion. Indeed, Villegas lost his PGA Tour playing rights in 2012. If you wander down the range at a Tour event, you will see a range of ages, body types, and levels of physical fitness.

The best players in the world struggle to play their best golf consistently even with the quantity of psychological advice and information available to them. It isn't unusual to see the world's best players shoot 65 one day, followed by 75 the next. Tiger Wood's greatest asset at his peak was a calmness and mental resilience which allowed him to produce his best golf when it mattered most, regardless of the apparent pressures of the situation.

How can Adam Scott, lauded as perhaps the best swinger of a golf club in the world, lose a four shot lead over the last four holes of the 2012 Open Championship? He played sublime golf for the previous three and a half rounds. Watching the television footage, there's no discernible change in his golf swing or putting stroke. I doubt Adam himself can explain exactly what happened at Royal Lytham on that July afternoon. I'm sure he believed in himself, trusted his swing, visualised the shot and went through his pre shot routine. He still couldn't par any of the last four holes.

Why is it that some of the 15 handicappers who turn up at my studio can regularly hit a driver 250 yards into a fairway, can repeatedly land a seven iron on a green from 150 yards and can hole a dozen four footers in a row on the practice green, but struggle to break 90 when they have a medal card in their hand?

Golfers are offered endless streams of technical information supposedly to help them improve, but they don't. They're told what to learn in terms of swing technique, but very little about how to learn it. They are overloaded with technical information and stuff to think about. This is counter productive, particularly when it comes to the mental side of golf which is such a significant aspect of the game.

They are then offered strategies and tips to manage their thinking, or cope with 'pressure'. Sometimes these tips work, but often they don't. Even if they do work, relief is temporary. Golfers are rarely, if ever, asked to look inwards, towards what might be causing them to feel 'pressure' in the first place.

Who is this book for?

I'm guessing you aren't completely happy with your game. Maybe you aren't enjoying it as much as you used to, or you have had some lessons and haven't improved as you had hoped? Maybe you're feeling stressed and under pressure when you play, and are looking for ways to cope with those feelings? Maybe you feel the progress in your game has levelled off, and you're looking for a way to improve your scores without another round of 'worse before it gets better' swing changes?

I'd love this book to be the catalyst for a new way of seeing things. Instead of searching for another swing model, another coach, new golf clubs, the latest training aid, more balls at the driving range, or a new fitness programme, I'd like this book to point you inwards.

How do you feel when you're playing golf? Where are those feelings coming from?

Are you relaxed, calm, decisive, resilient and free when you play? Or are you tight and pressured, a bundle of nerves? Are you anxiously waiting for the wheels to come off at the worst possible moment, as seems to happen more often than not?

I hope this book will prompt you to question your perceptions of the game. How does it look to you? When things are going well, golf seems simple and logical, make or miss. The problems start when we start digging deeper. Modern coaching seems to be pushing us towards playing and learning in a much more mechanical, scientific way. But can it really be boiled down to physics and ballistics, to analysis of the numbers?

I will suggest some ideas which may seem confusing, contradictory, baffling, paradoxical even, about the nature of reality, of time and space, and about ourselves. What we know, what we think we know and what we don't know.

Golf is played by fallible, emotional, sometimes irrational human beings, on the surface of a planet which is alive, ever changing, and unpredictable. This ball of rock was formed several billion years ago and then shaped by forces much more powerful than we can possibly imagine.

We launch a small, spherical projectile into the elements with hope and faith that it will fall in a way that will please us. That optimism is essential, but we also cherish the uncertainty. If we knew exactly what was going to happen after each swing, the game would lose its attraction very quickly.

Why is this paradox so appealing? Why are games so important to human beings? We have played them for at least the last few thousand years, almost certainly longer. What does playing golf do for us and on what level? Games are not essential to human existence, but I know that my life and that of many others would be significantly poorer without them.

Why are Golfers and Golf Struggling?

Golf is at a crossroads. The number of people playing is levelling off, if not falling. The demographic of golfers is aging, with fewer youngsters coming into the game. There are numerous theories put forward for this decline, from slow play to the cost of playing. From the lack of leisure time, to the game being difficult to learn.

I think all these opinions are missing the point. Golfers play golf because they love it. They enjoy it. It's challenging, it's fun. Unfortunately, the people who run the game and golfers themselves are largely oblivious to where our feelings of enjoyment come from. In the same way they look outside themselves for ways to improve their golf, they look outside for the reasons golf makes them happy, or unhappy, and for the reasons why they play golf at all.

The theory that the way to attract more people to the

game is to make it easier, less challenging, doesn't make sense. I've seen young children learn to hit the ball well in a couple of hours. Mastering something difficult is one of the most satisfying experiences a human being can have. It's why millions of golfers play on into their dotage. The challenge of golf is what keeps people coming back.

This book introduces three psychological principles which are the building blocks of the human experience. These principles offer explanations for the three big difficulties golfers seem to have. Learning and improving naturally without struggling. Playing their best golf when they really want to, and enjoying the game now and into the future.

I believe in fifty years time these principles will be accepted and be at the forefront of everyday psychological education, in the same way that germ theory led to hand washing and sterilisation of instruments being at the forefront of modern medical education. I believe sport and golf in particular, due to its individual, deliberate and cerebral nature, present a huge opportunity to help bring this understanding into the public consciousness.

The nature of these three principles is the truth, or as close to it as I have come. I just don't see how human beings can experience life in any other way. I don't imagine for a moment I see the nature of it as deeply as Sydney Banks, whose enlightenment experience in the autumn of 1973 led to this breakthrough, or as clearly as my friends and mentors Garret Kramer and Jamie Smart do.

I do see very clearly what these principles mean to me. I see their potential to make the game I love more enjoyable for those that play it, and more accessible for those that would like to play. I believe a new approach can change the experience of golf forever for my fellow golfers, without whose company the game would not be half the fun it is.

The game of golf is not the issue. Most golfers don't know where their feelings are coming from, so they have no idea why golf can feel so disappointing and frustrating sometimes. By the end of this book you will understand how your mind works and why you feel the way you do about the game. Why on some days you love it, on others it drives you crazy.

You will be amongst a select group of golfers who do understand, and you will see why these lucky golfers want to keep playing for as long as they can walk.

As a result of the understanding I'm about to share, you will play your best golf more often. You will find it easier to ride the inevitable mental challenges that the game throws at you. You will continue to learn and improve for as long as you choose to keep playing this amazing game. You will fall in love with the game all over again.

CHAPTER 2

Ups And Downs.

'It's a form of insanity to keep beating yourself over the head just because it feels good when you stop.'

—*John Geirach*

THIS IS MY STORY. It isn't the truth. It isn't reality. It's my recollections of the past thirty or so years of my life. This might sound like an odd distinction to make. You'll understand why I make it as the book progresses.

* * *

My golfing journey began at the age of twelve, chipping a golf ball around our back garden with Andrew Harrott, another young golfer who lived over the road. One afternoon, for some reason (possibly a bet) I was trying to hit a wedge over my parent's house from the back to the front garden.

Not for the last time in my golfing life, the occasion got to me. I tightened up and thinned it towards the kitchen window. I had time to wonder which of my parents would injure me most seriously when the ball hit the wooden frame between the two panes of glass and rebounded back to my feet. Three inches either way and I mightn't be writing these words. My golfing career would probably have been over before it began. Luck plays a significant part in the game of golf, as any major winner will tell you.

Over the next couple of years, I played at Mowsbury Park, the municipal course in Bedford during the summer holidays. I had some talent, but my technique was unconventional. I had a strong grip and a funky swing, but was good around the greens. I loved the feeling of hitting the ball, watching it soar off into space. Every round was an opportunity to learn, to improve and find out how well I could play. Golf was a fascinating challenge, a chance to compete and have fun with my mates.

My hero was Severiano Ballesteros, the legendary Spaniard. In his prime, Seve was the most exciting, naturally gifted player the world has ever seen. The obvious pleasure he got from the game inspired me. I loved the way he charged around the course, the joy he got from playing outrageous shots from impossible situations. I was completely hooked. I gave up football, rugby and athletics and just played golf.

Aged fifteen I joined Bedford and County Golf Club, where Chris Harrott, Andrew's father was the junior organiser. My first handicap was twenty three. I got down to scratch by the time I was eighteen. I still had a strong grip and hit it about 220 yards off the tee with a little fade. My strengths were confidence, persistence and the fact I possessed a short game that could get the ball up and down out of a rubbish bin. I took some lessons, practised hard and gradually improved my swing and ball striking.

I joined Woburn Golf Club in 1989 and represented Berkshire, Buckinghamshire and Oxfordshire at county level, combining golf with working at the American Golf Discount store in Biggleswade. Long hours in the golf shop didn't give me time to practice, so I jumped at the chance when my friend Bob Smith offered me a job as a sales agent for his golf accessories company. I racked up the miles around the Home Counties selling logoed ball markers and bag tags, Cape Crest Rainwear, Rhythm Clothing and Yonex golf clubs.

The highlight of my amateur career was reaching the final of the English Amateur Championship at Hunstanton in 1995. The match was an anti-climax. Mark Foster (subsequently a winner on the European Tour) beat me 6 & 5. Despite the loss, the English Golf Union gave me the opportunity to play for England in a tournament in Greece that September. It was a proud moment.

I was included in the national training squad that winter. At the first session, I had my swing analysed on video for the first time. I was mortified. It looked dreadful, nothing like I imagined. Coach Keith Williams suggested a number of changes to improve my ball striking. This was the start of fifteen years of swing changes with a number of different instructors. I wish I knew then what I know now.

Feeling The Pressure.

I turned professional in 1998 and secured a provisional

card to play the Australian PGA Tour that winter. There was Monday qualifying every week to get into tournaments. My nerves got the better of me more often than not.

I returned home in the spring of 1999 to play various mini tours. The Hippo Tour, the Futures Tour and the Players Tour were basically big sweepstakes where players put up the prize money rather than sponsors. The top ten finishers and the tournament organisers kept most of it. A back injury saved me from going completely broke, but put me out of the game for two years.

During my break from golf I married my girlfriend Belinda and we bought a house. I rediscovered my boyhood love of salmon fishing, helped Peter Little set up the EuroPro Tour, before taking a sales role with a software company. Recovery from injury and having forgotten how hard golf could be, I started playing again in 2002. I played full seasons on the EuroPro Tour in 2003, 2004 and 2005. I managed a few top ten finishes and ranked in the top 50 on the order of merit a couple of times. I entered European Tour Qualifying School on three or four occasions between 1998 and 2006, but never managed to play my best golf when I wanted or needed to.

I called time on my first playing career in 2006. Unsurprisingly, Belinda decided she'd had enough of sharing her life with a grumpy, broke, neurotic golf professional. Having followed me around the world paying more than her fair share of the bills and putting her life and career on hold, she gave me a choice: golf or her. The arguments that followed are some of my worst memories. We decided to go our separate ways a few weeks later. My dear friends Mike and Hannah Pilgrim offered me some work on their farm while I figured out what I could do with the rest of my life. I was pretty low and I'm not sure what would have happened if they hadn't been there for me.

My strongest memory of playing tournaments was feeling sick with nerves pretty much every time I teed it up. I was happiest when I was practising. I loved hitting golf balls and working on my swing or short game. Practising wasn't accompanied by the pressure I felt when playing.

The sad thing for me was, the better I got the less enjoyable the game seemed. My good rounds didn't give me much satisfaction. I was just doing what I expected. I took my poor rounds very personally, replaying the bad shots over and over in my mind. I felt I was a disappointment to all the people who were supporting me. This increased the nervous anxiety. In tournaments I felt I was battling, trying hard, and grinding. It felt like walking through a minefield, just waiting for something bad to happen, rather than doing something I loved. When I did have a good round, it felt more of a relief than a cause for celebration.

Looking back now, I had completely lost touch with the reasons I fell in love with the game when I was a kid. I had gone from playing golf for its own sake, the simple game of hitting a ball around a nicely manicured piece of countryside till it went in a hole, to playing another game

I had no chance of winning.

At the time I didn't understand what was happening. I just knew when I played badly I felt sad, disappointed, frustrated and angry. The tighter and more anxious I felt, the worse I played, which made me more tense, which made me play worse. A classic downward spiral.

I was trying to live up to my own expectations. I was trying to prove something to myself, my wife and our families and friends. I was trying to earn a living. Golf had become the means to an end, rather than something I did because I enjoyed it. Every shot was judged either good or bad depending on how it would affect other things in my life. I didn't appreciate a good swing for the great feeling it gave me, or a poor one as something I could learn from. Golf stopped being something I loved and became a job. The outcome had become more important than the process. The game wasn't fun any more. I came very close to giving up.

'Two Shots From Being Crazy'.

As the son of an author, I have always loved reading. A golfer has plenty of books to choose from. One of my favourites is 'Extraordinary Golf' by Fred Shoemaker. He makes an astute observation about the thinking the majority of golfers adopt once they've played the game for more than a few weeks. He calls this mind-set the 'Culture of Golfers'. Two particular statements perfectly describe my state of mind for most of my time as a tour professional.

The first is that all golfers, regardless of their ability

or status, are two bad shots away from being crazy.

The second is that most golfers believe that there is something wrong with their game or golf swing. They need to fix it in order to be happy with their golf.

This isn't just true of club golfers. A number of friends I grew up with are currently playing on the European Tour. Others are caddies or rules officials, or agents or coaches to tour players. The following statement might surprise club golfers: Shoemaker's Culture of Golfers is strong even at the highest levels of the game. It is hard to believe the level of insecurity amongst top players, their coaches and caddies.

The world's best golfers have weeks where they are two bad shots from going crazy in the same way most club players are. A minority would profess satisfaction with the way they're playing. They are always trying to improve their game or trying to fix something. Few would tell you they enjoy the game as much as they did when they were growing up.

There are many accounts of tour players who have won a major championship, then tried to change their swing or fix something in order to improve, or to get to 'the next level'. Usually they disappear from the limelight as their game deserts them. Martin Kaymer did it after winning the 2010 US PGA Championship. Clearly there wasn't much wrong with his golf, yet he believed his game wasn't complete, that it still wasn't good enough and needed fixing. He decided to change something that worked in the quest to get better. Michael Campbell and David Duval are other examples of players who went missing in action after major wins.

This is the paradox that makes the game so seductive and in many cases so addictive. Golf is difficult. It always looks like we can and indeed must improve. No one ever plays a round of golf where they don't think of shots they wish they could have again. We are always striving to get better. Unfortunately this striving often takes us in the opposite direction.

Teacher Fix Thyself.

Thankfully my love for the game returned once I stopped thinking that playing golf was my only means of making something of my life. I began teaching. It was fun helping other people play better and enjoy their golf. I began to remember the reasons I played the game in the first place.

Unfortunately, many golfers I meet are in a bad place psychologically for the same reasons I was. They have forgotten why they fell in love with golf, and are struggling to find any enjoyment in it. They play in the hope that the next round will be where it all turns round, like a gambler chasing his losses. Usually they are searching for technical improvements in the hope that better scores will rekindle their enthusiasm for the game. My experiences help me empathise, to see things from their perspective and to perhaps explain why that perspective isn't helping.

Sometimes the universe moves in ways we don't understand until we look back later.

Over the past thirty years, I've seen few different

ways of swinging a golf club. Some of them work better than others. I've experimented with some of them, persevered and played well with one or two. One thing I have learned from watching good players, is that a talented athlete can make any swing model work if they believe in it and practice it enough.

Maybe someone someday will come up with The One. The single, most efficient biomechanically correct way of swinging a golf club that everyone can use, regardless of size, shape, body type, strength, flexibility and athleticism. I'm not holding my breath for it, because there will always be personal preference and subjectivity involved.

When someone does find that optimal swing, they also need to explain to golfers that we have a natural way of learning new movement instead of working against our instincts as we seem to do at the moment. We need to accept that a person's golf swing will change and feel different from day to day, month to month, year to year, because we are human beings, and we change over time.

I have worked with some very good coaches during my playing days; Luther Blacklock, Chuck Quinton, Lee Scarbrow, Charlie Earp, Eddie Bullock, Kevyn Cunningham, Alex Hay, Keith Williams, Tommy Horton and others. The lessons I learnt from them may not have been the ones they thought they were teaching me, but proved to be valuable nonetheless.

I have played my best golf when I felt I understood my own golf swing enough that I didn't need to think about it. I may have come to that understanding through studying other swing models, but my biggest steps forward have come through increased awareness of what I was actually doing. Awareness of what felt good in my swing and what didn't. I don't think it's coincidence that some of the all time great ball strikers – Hogan, Snead, Trevino, George Knudsen and Moe Norman, for example – were mainly self-taught.

I have been fortunate to play with a number of fantastic golfers over the years. You may have heard of Retief Goosen, Luke Donald, Paul Casey, David Howell, Mark Foster, Justin Rose, Andrew Coltart, Ian Poulter and Lee Westwood. I also played with a number of talented golfers who never made it onto the big stage. David Fisher, Charlie Challen, Garry Harris and Gordon Sherry were all huge talents who could easily have become household names. I've spent many hours wondering about what separates those who went on to play golf at the highest level and those of us who are now doing something else. I imagine they have too.

The understanding I'm about to share points to some of the answers. The secret, if you want to call it that, is something you can't see. A clear head, an inner resilience and a deep sense of awareness are more important than a technically perfect golf swing or a repeatable putting stroke.

I wish the golf instruction industry would change its focus from teaching technique, to helping golfers understand how they can play their best golf more often. Two of the most important books I've read about learning golf, 'The Inner Game of Golf' by Tim Gallwey and

Shoemaker's 'Extraordinary Golf', emphasise that how we learn is much more important than what we learn.

Unfortunately the instruction industry seems obsessed with perfecting the golf swing, rather than with understanding, functionality and enjoyment. This obsession has led to large numbers of unhappy and frustrated golfers, many of whom are leaving the game and looking for other things to do in their leisure time.

Learning movement is a natural process we all do from the moment we are born. It doesn't need to be broken down, packaged up as a seven step plan and marketed on the internet with a new training aid. Until we accept this and point golfers in the direction of instinctive learning, golfers will continue to find improving their golf swings a frustrating, uphill battle.

Welcome to the Madhouse.

The feelings of insecurity, nervousness and anxiety I struggled with for most of my golfing life are not uncommon. Over the years I sought advice from a number of sports psychologists to help me feel more at ease when I played. Teaching the mental side of golf has been a big growth area in the last thirty years, with a number of books written on the subject.

'Golf is not a Game of Perfect' by Bob Rotella was published in May 1995. In August of that year I reached the final of the English Amateur Championship, probably my finest golfing achievement. I remember reading Rotella's book and adopting a few of his techniques, particularly for the short game and putting. Picking a small target and letting the shot go without delay were two I remember adopting. I practiced my short game a lot leading up to the tournament, and putted like a demon that week. The greens were hard and super fast. I holed yards and yards of putts right up until the final match.

I have always been a good match play golfer. The idea that a poor shot might only cost me one hole seemed to reduce the pressure and anxiety I experienced compared to stroke play tournaments.

I went to see sports psychologist Jack Lamport Mitchell shortly before travelling up to Hunstanton in Norfolk. In my initial assessment, he scored me one out of ten for ability to relax, five out of ten for self-confidence, four out of ten for muscle tension and one out of ten for dealing with competition nerves. He sent a lovely letter of congratulations after the final which I still have.

He gave me a relaxation tape to listen to, and showed me a deep breathing exercise I could use. I remember feeling nervous as usual, but I coped and enjoyed a couple of matches. I played against a good friend, Lewis Watcham in the last sixteen and Jim Miller from Yorkshire in the quarterfinals.

I made two outrageous up and downs over the last three holes of the semi-final. One from a bad lie in a greenside bunker on the sixteenth, the other from the first tee beside the final green, where Shaun Webster kindly three putted from the front fringe to give me the win.

Getting to the final was the best result of my golfing

life. I thought I had made a breakthrough with regards to my anxiety, now that I had a couple of tricks up my sleeve to cope with it. I kept listening to the tape, and doing the breathing exercise. I worked hard on developing and improving my pre shot routine as Rotella recommended, focussing on a small target and visualising the ball going towards it.

Despite following the advice, my anxious feelings returned and never really went away. My golf stayed pretty much at the same level rather than continuing on an upward trajectory. Over the following years I went to see a number of other mind coaches with similar results. They gave me the latest strategy, all variations on the same theme of analysing my thinking and coping with the feelings. Sometimes I felt better and played well for a while, but then returned to how I was feeling before; stressed out and increasingly frustrated.

I've spoken to many golfers about their experiences with sports psychologists and mind coaches. Sometimes they play well after the session, sometimes they don't. When they do, there seems to be a reason for it. However, doing the same thing next time doesn't lead to the same feeling or level of performance.

Relaxation techniques such as deep breathing, muscle flexing, rapid eye movements, thinking about a happy time or place, may all relieve tension or anxiety levels in the short term. Visualisation can work, but only if you're not too anxious or tense to visualise. What happens if other scenarios keep coming into mind rather than the ones you want to see?

I remember one well meaning psychologist who wanted to take me back to memories of past rounds where I had played badly in order to deal with the feelings those memories triggered. I remember thinking at the time, 'This seems a bit cruel and unnecessary. How can reliving bad memories help make me play better in the future?'

It just bought all the old feelings back. I was then supposed to get rid of the anxiety by tapping my finger on my face and forehead.

When a golfer goes to see a sports psychologist, he or she expects to get a technique or a strategy to work on. Most begin by analysing the content of a person's thinking in order to explain feelings or behaviour. They then offer a routine or a practice to mitigate or replace the unwanted feelings and thus change the behaviour.

Unfortunately, this is a complete misunderstanding of how the mind actually works, and is usually more harmful than helpful. I have yet to see or hear of a successful technique, routine or strategy which works successfully on every shot. Maybe I'm missing the point. Many sports psychologists seem to be making a good living from what they're prescribing.

Time for a New Approach.

I'm a relatively intelligent person and a decent golfer, probably in the top one or two percent of everyone playing the game worldwide. I've played sub par golf for the past twenty five years, won my club championship five times, represented my county and my country, and reached the final of my national championship. I earn a proportion of my living every year from playing golf in professional tournaments.

However, in the past I rarely played my best golf when I really wanted to. I came very close to giving up the game because it seemed to be making me miserable. When I'm teaching, I see first hand the difficulties other people have trying to play their best golf consistently. I regularly see both the enjoyment and the frustration the game can bring.

Despite my struggles, I consider myself very fortunate to have had the opportunity to follow my dream. I've played some of the best golf courses around the world, met some wonderful people, many of whom I'm proud to call my friends. I wouldn't swap a single hour I spent on the range and the putting green, from junior golf right through to professional level.

I have hit hundreds of thousands of golf balls and tried many different ways of swinging a golf club. I have developed a deep understanding of how my golf swing works. I'm currently hitting the ball better than ever and I'm looking forward to playing some good golf in the coming months and years.

By far the most important thing I've learnt is the understanding I'm going to share with you in the following pages. It provides an explanation for my difficulties playing my best golf when I really wanted to and the obsession I had with constantly changing and fixing my golf swing. It led me to the breakthrough where I saw where my feelings of anxiety and frustration were really coming from.

How To Read This Book.

This might seem like an odd instruction. Hopefully it will stop you falling into the same mental trap which caught me when I began to see the possibilities this understanding offers. Like you might be doing now, I was searching for something. When we are searching for an answer, we read and listen in a particular way. We read with our intellect, rather than with an open mind. We filter and judge and compare what we are reading to see if it stacks up against what we already know or believe.

What you won't get from this book is an intellectual understanding of how to play golf. If you start to feel excited or agitated, please put it down for a while. What I hope you experience is a nice, calm, relaxed feeling as you read. This is the first clue that it is reaching the parts other golf books have failed to reach.

That's the feeling of your connection to your inner wisdom opening up, of your thinking slowing down. If you get this feeling, you're on the right track. If you start asking yourself questions about how to apply the things you read here, or feeling that you want to rush out to try and put them into practice, you've probably missed it.

If this doesn't make sense to you at the moment, don't worry. It didn't when I first heard it either. I promise, if you can read the rest of the book with an open mind and a good feeling, what I'm about to tell you can't help but have the same positive effect on your golf as it has had on mine.

CHAPTER 3

Why Isn't Golf Fun Any More?

'Of all the hazards, fear is the worst.'

—*Bobby Jones*

THE LAST TIME I FAILED to get through the first stage of European Tour Qualifying School, I remember walking off the final green and the question above popped into my head. (I think my answer was 'Because you're so crap at it.') I didn't understand the haphazard, ephemeral nature of Thought at that point, so I took it a lot more seriously than I would do now. I wrote down more answers when I got home.

Looking back on those answers now, it seems like whiny, self centred introspection. But as I started teaching and talking to more golfers about how they felt after they played, what they were telling me sounded very familiar.

If I went round the lounge at Woburn Golf Club on a Saturday lunchtime and discreetly asked: 'Who honestly enjoyed their round this morning?' I would suggest fewer than half the people would answer positively. Woburn is a beautiful place to play. It has three of the best courses in the country, always in excellent condition.

The members are friendly, welcoming and play golf in good spirit. So why are there so many frustrated people in the room? They spend a lot of time and money on their hobby. Why are so few of them enjoying themselves?

What Do Golfers Want?

In 'The Inner Game of Golf', Tim Gallwey suggests golfers want three different things from their experience. He illustrates these desires in an infographic which he calls the 'Performance, Enjoyment, Learning triangle' (P.E.L).

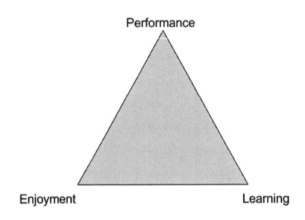

He suggests that balancing up the three sides of the triangle is essential for a golfer to perform well, fulfil their potential by improving skills and technique, enjoy what they are doing and get satisfaction from it. The 'Inner Game' has become a huge coaching business. This infographic is the foundation of the philosophy behind it.

P.E.L makes sense to me. From my own experience of playing, and from talking to a few hundred golfers over the past five years, there is truth in it. In all my conversations, enjoyment is the overwhelming priority for golfers. They want to have a good time when they play, to feel their investment of time and money has been worth it. The problem is they don't seem to know what that means or where the enjoyment comes from. I started off playing for fun, but I got confused as my game got better. Shooting 68 should always be fun, but often it felt like hard work.

Gallwey comes to a similar conclusion, that most golfers are confused. They place far more emphasis on performance than the other two areas. They believe that playing better than their expectations will bring enjoyment. Many golfers feel they only enjoy golf when their performance matches predetermined levels. That was certainly true in my case.

This mindset creates an unwinnable game. The better I played, the higher my expectations became. If I was designing a process to make myself miserable, it would be hard to come up with a more successful one.

Most golfers tell a similar story. They want to play close to their potential 'best golf' most of the time. They especially want to play well when they consider a round to be important. They also want to learn and improve. They want their golf swing to become more efficient. They want to learn to control the golf ball better, to hit it further, to improve their scores and lower their handicap as their golf career progresses.

Golfers want to enjoy learning and playing. They want the process of improvement to feel free and fun, rather than grinding and turning golf into another form of work. Our thoughts about what we want from the game will change from day to day and moment to moment. This is normal and completely natural, but confusing for many golfers. They don't understand why they enjoy golf one day and not the next, despite the fact they might have shot a similar score.

In theory it should be easier than ever to improve, to play well and shoot good scores. Equipment today is more forgiving and easier to use than thirty years ago. It can be adjusted minutely to suit every aspect of our golf swings. Golf courses are maintained to higher standards and practice facilities such as driving ranges are more accessible.

Technology in the form of high speed video cameras and launch monitors give us endless accurate feedback about our swings. Yet handicaps aren't coming down. Participation is flat, if not falling, and enjoyment seems to be in short supply at most golf clubs I visit.

Why am I Shaking?

When I was playing tournaments, every time I stepped on the first tee with a scorecard in my hand, my default state was stressed out. Fear became normal. Most golfers will recognise the feelings: a physical reaction in the form of tightness in the stomach and in the small muscles of the hands and arms. Most golfers will also have come to the same conclusion as I did – it's hard to play your best golf when you're shaking, and it isn't much fun. I much preferred practising to playing. I didn't feel nervous and I hit the ball much better when I had a big bucket of practice balls in front of me.

A successful golf swing is dependent on good timing. Good golfers don't hit bad shots because their technique suddenly failed them. After all, the same swing hit good shots when they were relaxed. A bad shot happens because their timing, the sequencing of their swing, was slightly off. Variations in sequencing can change the clubface angle, the clubhead path or the low point of the golf swing.

Tightness and tension affects timing. Small alterations in timing causes inconsistent golf shots. I spent thousands of hours on the practice ground trying to build a golf swing that would stand up under pressure. Unfortunately it isn't golf swings that fail under pressure. People who don't understand the nature of Thought often fail under pressure.

We Know What to Do, We Just Don't Do It.

Most golfers who have been playing the game for a while, know what they should do to play well. They know how to grip the golf club, how to align themselves to the target and where the ball should be in their stance. They have a reasonable understanding about how they want to swing the golf club. Unfortunately, many golfers don't do the things they need to do to play well. Even worse, they don't even know they aren't doing them, because their awareness of what they *are actually doing* is so low.

There are few things more needless than missing the fairway or green because you haven't lined up correctly.

I see this all the time when I play in Pro Ams or give playing lessons. The golfer aims twenty yards off line. They swing well, they hit the ball solidly and they hit it straight, but it finishes in the rough. Poor alignment can be more damaging than just missing greens. If your body isn't aimed properly you will make swing compensations to start the ball on target. The swing you're using on the course is different from the one you have been practising. No wonder something doesn't feel right.

I know a number of golfers who set up to the ball with a good grip, but move their hands on the club at the last second. When the ball goes left or right and I ask them why, they don't even realise they have changed their grip. They know how to hold the club but they don't do it properly.

Reviewing the notes I used to make after each tournament round, I am amazed at the number of times I wrote down the same things. I made the same mistakes over and over again. I'm not stupid, but my notes suggest I used to play golf like I was. I knew what I should do, but I didn't do it consistently because my consciousness was low most of the time.

Are You Playing Golf Swing, or Playing Golf?

One reason golfers don't play well as often as they would like, is because they don't appreciate the difference between learning a golf swing and performing it. Performance means playing your best golf regularly, when you really want to. Learning is changing or refining a movement pattern (a golf swing) to make it more efficient. Learning is best done away from the golf course, in an environment where you can think consciously about what you are doing, make mistakes, experiment with different ways of moving and get feedback.

I used to write down my swing thought for the day on my yardage chart. I've got dozens of them, all with different things I was working on each week. Some of the books have got four or five thoughts for the same round. I spent a huge amount of mental energy judging how well I reproduced my swing technique. This was a distraction from the real task of getting the ball in the hole in the fewest number of strokes possible. As I discovered, nobody will pay you for having a pretty golf swing, hitting the ball with a nice draw or hitting a certain number of greens in regulation.

When we set out to play an important round, the game should be shooting the lowest score possible. Yet we distract ourselves with trying to swing 'correctly' or put into practice what we were learning in our last lesson. We go into 'Swing Fix' mode as soon as we hit one bad shot, rather than forgetting about it and moving on to the next one.

Not so Great Expectations.

Golf is a bit different from other leisure activities. We have a black and white way of judging how we perform every time we play. I don't keep score when I'm fishing or skiing, but I know few golfers who play without knowing their score. Most have a handicap they use to judge how they are doing against the course, against other golfers and against themselves. They have a number in their head before they tee off. If they are close to that number then they feel they have enjoyed the round. If they are a long way over their target, then it might well be a tense conversation at the bar afterwards.

Here is a summary of the game most of us play instead of golf. You make up an arbitrary target you need to achieve in order to be happy. If you don't reach that target, you must beat yourself up about it. If you reach your goal, immediately make up another target which is more difficult to achieve. Repeat until you are so fed up with golf that gardening begins to look like an attractive alternative.

This is the 'I'll be Happy When Game'. There are some interesting variations of it at the end of the chapter.

When they aren't thinking about what they need in order to be happy, many golfers think about what they don't want in order not to be miserable. They worry about looking silly in front of their friends and peers. They worry about being embarrassed by their technique or their scores. They worry about what other people think about them.

They have a variation of the same negative mind-set when they are standing over a shot. They dwell on where they don't want to hit the ball, and are so focused on preventing a bad shot that the possibility of hitting a good one doesn't even occur to them.

Why is it so Hard to Get Better?

When most golfers are at the range or practice ground, they are judging themselves on how well they are hitting the ball, rather than learning or refining their technique. The success of a session is judged in terms of 'Did I strike the ball as I believe I should, and did the ball go where I wanted it to go?'

The purpose of practice is to learn and develop your golf swing. Instead, I would constantly judge myself. I used to stand in the same place hitting the same club to the same target in the same way. I was happy if I hit a good shot and angry if I hit a bad one. There wasn't a lot of learning going on, just a lot of judging. I often see people getting annoyed and berating themselves on driving ranges. It's highly amusing – if you don't have to go home with them afterwards.

The mind and body learn as much from bad golf shots as from good ones. We learn to walk by falling over. We learn to ride a bike by wobbling around and bouncing off the stabilisers. We learn to catch by dropping the ball. We learn motor skills by trying, failing, trying again, failing better, trying again and again until we get it. Except with golf. With golf we try, we fail, we try, we fail again. We have a think. We go onto YouTube or order a book or a DVD, or we find someone to tell us what we are doing wrong and how they think we should fix it.

You Can't Fix it if You Don't Know What's Broken.

Fred Shoemaker makes the observation that the first step

to changing and improving your golf swing is attaining a high level of awareness for what you already do. I'm surprised when I ask golfers during a lesson what something in their swing feels like. Many of them reply: 'I don't know.'

Golfers struggle to learn for exactly the same reason they struggle to play well. They don't have awareness of what they are doing while they are doing it. If you can't feel it, you will really struggle to change it or improve it, because you aren't aware of the difference between the movement you make now, and the one you want to make.

Too Much Information.

Modern golfers suffer from information overload. There is so much dissection and analysis of the golf swing available in instruction books, magazines, online articles and YouTube videos, that they struggle to put it all into context. I know mid handicap golfers who would easily pass a written exam on the golf swing. They know about swing plane, swing path, angle of attack, weight shift, pronation, supination, getting stuck and coming over the top. They just aren't sure how it all applies to them. A statement I hear regularly is;

'I understand the (pick one of many) swing model and how it works, I just don't really know how where my swing is in relation to it.'

All their knowledge is irrelevant because they have no idea how to put it into practice. A map isn't much use if you don't know your present location.

We Were Born to Learn.

Human beings have evolved to become the fastest most efficient learners of new skills on the planet. We are natural learners from the minute we are born. Learning is an innate ability that never leaves us. Unfortunately, when it comes to learning movement as adults this is forgotten. We have tried to intellectualise and sanitise the process, to cut out mistakes and make it as risk free as possible. The fear of looking silly drives us more than the desire to learn and improve.

Learning a new movement pattern seems clumsy, chaotic, muddled, is definitely not linear and can occasionally be painful, as anyone with children will know. In golf, we have tried to eliminate the clumsy chaotic stages by trying to make it a thinking, rather than a doing and feeling process.

Some of the biggest eureka moments in my golf swing have come in a twenty minute practice session doing something counter intuitive, like exaggerating a very flat swing plane, or feeling the club head accelerate after the ball rather than before it. Conversely, I have spent months making thousands of repetitions of the same position in the swing, only to review a video of actually hitting a ball and having it look exactly the same. Repetition has its place, but it works far better with increased awareness.

If it Ain't Broke........

So far the responsibility has been on the golfer, but the golf instruction industry has to take some of the blame.

Some golf coaches and teachers are seen and like to be seen as 'experts,' as the owners and dispensers of knowledge and information. Golfers are seen as empty vessels to be filled up with this knowledge. Their transformation into better golfers will reflect well on the coach. It is a very Outside In model of teaching and learning, which is gradually being seen as archaic, outdated and largely ineffective.

There's a lovely story about the late, great Bob Torrance, father of Ryder Cup captain Sam and coach to numerous Tour players. Rory McIlroy was a young superstar with huge potential, (both talent and earning wise) who had just played in the Walker Cup and was about to turn professional. Michael Bannon had coached McIlroy since he was a boy and deserves credit for nurturing one of the best swings in golf.

Rory felt he wanted a fresh pair of eyes to look at his swing, so he flew up to Scotland to see Bob. On the practice ground at Largs, the young man went through the bag, hitting shot after pure shot. Bob stood watching, smoking a cigarette and as usual, saying very little. After finishing by smashing a few drivers into the distance, Rory turned and said, 'Well, what do you think?'

Bob paused for a moment, then growled back in his heavy brogue, 'I wouldna dream of touching that golf swing, and I din'na think you should let anyone else touch it either.'

He turned on his heel and set off towards the clubhouse.

The best coaches have a few things in common. They

don't fix what isn't broken. They ask lots of questions They don't try to impose their own ideas by telling you what to think and what to feel. They let you make mistakes and prompt you to find your own solutions. This is a much more productive way of learning than being given all the answers.

The 'I'll Be Happy When Game'.

Most golfers on the planet are playing a variation on this game. You might recognise it from other areas your life. Jamie Smart coined the phrase in his excellent book 'Clarity; Clearer Mind, Better Performance'.

As I described earlier, golfers have a list of things they believe they need to do, feel or achieve in order to get what they want from golf. It starts from the moment we first pick up a golf club and, for most people, ends when we can't play any more. See if any of the following sounds familiar?

I'll be Happy When... for Beginners.

'I'll be happy when I can hit the ball.'

'I'll be happy when I can hit the ball in the air.'

'I'll be happy when I can hit the ball further.'

'I'll be happy when I can hit the ball straight.'

I'll be Happy When... for Club Golfers.

'I'll be happy when I break 100, 90, 80, 70.'

'I'll be happy when I stop (pick one) shanking, slicing, hooking, topping the ball.'

'I'll be happy when I get my handicap into single figures.'

'I'll be happy when I win the club championship.'

'I'll be happy when I break par.'

'I'll be happy when I get to a scratch handicap.'

I'll be Happy When... for Professionals and Wannabe Professionals.

'I'll be happy when I'm playing golf for a living.'

'I'll be happy when I get my tour card.'

'I'll be happy when I keep my tour card.'

'I'll be happy when I win my first tour event.'

'I'll be happy when I make the Ryder Cup team.'

'I'll be happy when I win my first major championship.'

'I'll be happy when I prove that my first major wasn't a fluke.'

This game is unwinnable, as a few major champions would accept. Several winners of golf's biggest events have admitted to a feeling of emptiness after achieving the thing they had worked all their lives for.

The goal they were chasing never had the power to give them the feelings they were looking for in the first place, but they needed to achieve it for them to realise.

It Isn't Only Golfers.

I have few regrets about the years I spent chasing my dream. After all, it has brought me to the very happy situation I'm in now. The one thing I would change? I would love to have played a big tournament free from anxiety and stressful feelings. At the time, I thought it was just me who was suffering. Subsequent conversations with guys I played with over the years have revealed many of us felt the same.

It isn't only golfers. I have friends who played other sports professionally. It seems like fear and anxiety are familiar companions for many high level performers.

Matt Jackson has been one of my closest friends since we kicked a tennis ball around the playground at primary school. Matt was an outstanding footballer. He played for England under 21s, for eight different professional teams, made over one hundred and thirty appearances for Everton, including winning the 1995 F.A Cup final. He was the consummate professional, a student of the game. He trained hard, looked after himself and made sure he got the most out of his talent.

I remember sitting in the pub one evening a few weeks after he retired in 2008. We were the right side of a couple of steaks and few pints and were having a good chat. I asked him whether he missed football.

'Not really', he said. 'I couldn't be sitting here doing this if I was still playing.'

I was a bit surprised.

'So you don't miss the game? You don't miss playing in front of thirty thousand people every week?'

'I miss the craic with the lads at training, but I don't miss the game.'

'So you didn't enjoy it then?'

'I enjoyed it when the final whistle went if we had won. But I didn't enjoy the match itself. I think the last time I could honestly say I enjoyed a game of football was when I was about fourteen.'

'Why didn't you enjoy it?'

'Because I was always worried about playing badly, of making a mistake. The stakes were so high. I felt like peoples' livelihoods were dependent on how we played.'

I felt sad. Not in the sense I felt sorry for him. Matt has had a fantastic career. At forty years of age he had made a great living for him and his family. He can choose what he does for the rest of his days. It just struck me as a shame he had what most blokes would see as the ultimate career, yet he didn't enjoy playing the game he loved as a kid.

It seems to be accepted as a fact of life by most golfers and other athletes that 'pressure', feeling anxious and stressed out, is part of the deal. If you want to be successful, you have to learn to cope with it. No pain, no gain. In order to be successful, you have to suffer. It's assumed that the rewards make it all worthwhile.

In order to cope, with the pressure of the situation, it has become common practice to use techniques to help golfers cope with and overcome their feelings. I've tried most of them. They sometimes work, but if they do, relief is temporary.

Many of these strategies focus on the golfer's thoughts about the situation. They look for a logical explanation and encourage the golfer to think through each scenario so they can see that what they are worrying about isn't really scary and the feelings will go away. The advice is to replace the negative thought with a positive one. It sounds promising, but anyone who has attempted it will confirm how difficult it is to manage your thinking. Trying to find a logical explanation for every crazy situation your imagination can come up with is a never ending task.

Finding the Fun Again.

Golf has given me so much pleasure over the past thirty years. I don't want to give the impression that it's all doom and gloom. Many lucky players do enjoy their golf. I hope the rest of the book will help these golfers play better and get even more from it than they are doing now. The reason for writing this book is that many golfers find the things they think they want from the game elusive, whether that's more fun, a better swing or lower scores. They only play close to their potential occasionally, and rarely when they really want to.

Learning and improving proves difficult. Despite the improvements in equipment and condition of golf courses, the average handicap has hardly improved in the past thirty years. Enjoyment and fun are rare experiences, paradoxically particularly so for better players. Feelings of frustration, anxiety and disappointment are more common for many good golfers.

I am about to introduce you to a different way of seeing your golf. It's the answer to the question posed at the start of the chapter. Golf can be fun again, It should be fun. In the coming pages, you will see how a fundamental change in your perception can help you enjoy the game again, improve your technique, and play your best golf more often.

CHAPTER 4

Playing a Different Game.

'One of the greatest misconceptions ever, is the belief that it takes years to find wisdom. Many experience time, few experience wisdom. The achievement of mental stability and peace of mind is one thought away from everyone on earth...if you can find that one thought.'

—*Syd Banks*

IN DECEMBER 2011, I SAW the nature of the misunderstanding I had been living most of my life. I began to see why I had spent much of my golf career feeling anxious, and why I had similar feelings around other parts of my life, particularly relationships, work and money.

My life situation was changing significantly. I finished playing full time golf, and was working my way through the three-year qualification to become a member of the Professional Golfers Association. I was trying to build up my teaching business at a golf club struggling in difficult economic times. I got divorced, and watched my father lose his battle with cancer.

Just before Christmas I went to London to meet up with friends. We were sitting in a pub near Tottenham

Court Road on a Friday evening when I was introduced to Jamie Smart. He introduced himself as 'kind of a coach'.

Jamie asked me what I did for a living.

'I'm a golf pro', I replied.

'Oh Cool! My brother is a pro at Whistler in Canada. Are you playing on the Tour?'

'I played the Mini Tours for a while, but wasn't good enough to make the step up. I'm coaching now but still playing a bit.'

'Why didn't you make it?'

'I guess I wasn't good enough. I'm a decent player, but I don't play my best golf when I need to. I always feel anxious and tight when I'm under pressure.'

'What are you anxious about?'

The questions were starting to make me feel a bit self conscious, but there was something about Jamie's manner that gave me the feeling I could trust him.

'Playing badly, failing, not being good enough, letting myself and everybody else down. Not making any money.'

Then he said something that must have hit home, because I couldn't get it out of my mind.

'Sam, it's never the tournament, or money, or your score that makes you feel anxious or under pressure. What's actually making you feel scared is your own thinking.'

I stared into my pint for a couple of seconds, ruminating on the implications of what he had just said. A thought came to me.

'This bloke is mental. Well, either he is or I am..... I hope to God it's him.'

When I got home, the conversation kept coming back to me. It made no sense at an intellectual level, but something about Jamie's closing statement was having an intriguing effect. Somehow I felt calmer, more at ease with myself. I called him a few days later and we met up for coffee.

He gave me a book, 'StillPower' by Garret Kramer, signed by the author. Garret is a performance coach from New Jersey in the United States. His book is an account of his experiences working with ice hockey players, and more recently with other athletes and golfers. The two of them became my mentors. My perspective of my world changed in a matter of weeks.

The Outside In Illusion.

What I'm about to say might come as a surprise. It challenges our basic idea of what we think of as reality. My quest to become better at hitting a small white ball into a slightly larger hole has led me to explore some unusual places physically, mentally and spiritually.

The nature of this illusion is particularly puzzling until you see the implications of it. It was my big insight. I realised why life and golf had seemed such a struggle at times.

My nervous feelings didn't stem from the tournament, the scorecard, my golf swing, my financial situation, my relationships or from anywhere outside me. My feelings before and during tournaments, were coming 100% from my thinking at that moment, from a story I was making up about myself.

The truth is that none of what we feel as human beings comes from our situation or circumstances. Not from events or occurrences, from people, from lack of money, from bad shots or unlucky bounces, or from anything outside us.

The extent to which we see this fundamental truth, sometimes referred to as 'grounding', has the potential to change your life and your golf game in an instant. It is the answer to serious issues such as stress, anxiety, depression and addiction, let alone a fragile putting stroke, first tee nerves or a lost ball.

Please contemplate this truth for a second. Human beings create their experience of life from the Inside Out, rather than passively seeing and feeling what is happening from the Outside In. Don't worry if that sounds like double dutch at the moment. It will become clearer as this chapter unfolds.

This truth has profound implications for the question 'Why isn't golf fun any more?

When we attribute our feelings – whether it's feelings of fun, enjoyment, sadness, frustration or anger – to what we are doing or to our apparent success or failure, we are looking in the wrong direction. That simple misunderstanding makes us feel uncomfortable and uneasy because deep down in our heart of hearts, we know it isn't true.

If we go to play golf because we think a good round might make us 'better' than who we already are, the quiet voice of our common sense tells us we are trying to achieve something impossible. No wonder golf doesn't feel like fun when the game we are playing can't be won.

So does that mean we can't be happy when we play golf, that we can never have fun when we play?

Of course not. That would be as illogical as the premise above. The truth is we can be happy any time we play, regardless of how we're doing it and who we're doing it with.

It isn't about what we do. The spirit in which we play and the clarity of mind we experience will determine whether we enjoy the game or not.

If we understand this truth, we are free. Free to enjoy golf for what it really is; the most enjoyable, interesting, challenging game on earth. We play for fun, and hopefully we learn, expand our capabilities and improve. We play for the love of the game, rather than for approval, respect from others, prizes, fame or money.

As we go deeper, you'll learn that the degree to which we see the Inside Out understanding affects everything in our lives, not just golf. Everyone has their own reasons for doing whatever they do. Golf is no different. You might want to pause for a moment to ask yourself a question.

What are your reasons for playing? What gets you out on the course or the driving range?

Your thoughts before, during and after you play will be at the heart of why the game seems more enjoyable some days than others, and why it can be so hard to play well consistently. It's never down to the game itself.

You Don't Know What You Don't Know.

In the past, mankind has lived for lengthy periods where a misunderstanding or an illusion has been the commonly held view of 'reality'.

For example not so very long ago:

People believed the world was flat. They thought if you sailed over the horizon you fell off the edge of the earth into hell.

People believed the sun moved around the earth. They thought the sun rose in the east and set in the west. The idea of the earth spinning on its axis and moving around the sun was heresy.

People believed diseases and illnesses were caused by bad smells. They had no understanding of bacteria or germs. They carried bunches of flowers called posies to protect themselves against sickness.

People honestly and sincerely believed these misunderstandings, but they were never true. With hindsight, even with what we know today, it is possible to see how these ideas could be accepted as facts.

We get fooled by visual illusions even in today's connected, well-informed world. For example, I didn't know until recently there was a white arrow in the Federal Express Logo pictured below. (If you can't see it, look between the 'E' and the 'x'). The truth about any intellectual fact is that you don't know what you don't know.

You remain unaware until you get an insight, some fresh thinking which changes your perspective. A realisation that you didn't know. Even then you might remain sceptical until you actually see it for yourself. If I hadn't added the picture of the logo, just told you the arrow was there, you may have doubted until you Googled it.

To quote former US Secretary of Defence Donald Rumsfeld,

"There are known knowns. These are things we know that we know. There are known unknowns. That is to say, there are things that we know we don't know. But there are also unknown unknowns. There are things we don't know we don't know."

When you know something and it seems obvious, you tend to assume everyone else knows. If you always knew the arrow was in the logo, you assume everyone else sees it. You won't go round telling people. To quote Basil Fawlty, nobody wants to be known as 'master of the bleedin' obvious'. An object stays hidden in plain sight because people who see it assume everyone else sees it, so they don't speak out.

Maybe you know someone who seems calm, resilient, productive, humble and compassionate, who takes things in their stride. Their life seems to progress with ease and delight, regardless of circumstances. Some people are naturally 'grateful for their highs and graceful with their lows,' as psychologist George Pransky would say.

These people seem to know that circumstances have little bearing on how they feel, whether or not they know intellectually how the thought – feeling relationship works. They reasonably assume that it's the same for everyone, although they must wonder why the world seems such a crazy place sometimes. They don't shout about the fact that people or situations don't stress them out all that much, because to them that's just the way it is.

I mentioned that Ian Poulter doesn't get nervous when he plays golf, despite the tension we assume surrounds a particular shot or tournament. Ian instinctively knows the situation has no bearing on how he feels. I have no idea how he achieved this state of mind. I doubt he does either. I'm pretty sure he didn't discover it in a book, or hear it from a sports psychologist, a coach or another player. It's just something he knows intuitively. In his own words, he 'plays the shot, not the situation'.

People who don't see that their feelings come from their thinking, don't know that they don't know. It looks to them their feelings come from what is happening around them. They hang onto the highs, suffer the lows, fight their way through, struggle and cope. It's not until they realise the relationship between their feelings and their thoughts, that they see why life seemed so hard, and how different it can be. Sadly, a common response is 'it can't be that simple' and they continue to look outside themselves for answers, prolonging their suffering.

The Enlightenment Experience.

Sydney Banks left school at fifteen. He emigrated to Canada, where he worked as a welder in a paper mill. In the autumn of 1973, at the age of forty two, he had what he described as 'an enlightenment experience.' The realisation that his thinking was the source of his insecure feelings, took him from a depression he had suffered his whole life, to a state of peace and clarity. He saw the potential of his insight, and knew he had to share his experience with the world. Banks is acknowledged as the man who first raised awareness of the Three Principles of Mind, Consciousness and Thought. He wrote a number of articles and books and gave speeches and lectures all over the world.

For centuries there has been awareness of the truth that how we feel comes from Thought. Over two thousand years ago, Greek philosophers Aristotle and Plotinus pointed to the fact happiness comes from within.

'Happiness depends on ourselves'.

—*Aristotle*

'there exists no single human being that does not either potentially or effectively possess this thing we hold to constitute happiness.'

—*Plotinus*

All the main religions and philosophies point us 'inside' in our search for happiness, peace and meaning in our lives, towards our natural human instincts for love, caring, and cooperation, towards spiritual wisdom, rather than outside towards possessions, achievements and validation from others.

The quote at the start of this chapter is from Banks' book 'The Missing Link'. It suggests that no matter how low our state of mind, a simple piece of fresh thinking can change how we feel in an instant. We are only ever one thought away from peace, contentment and happiness. The insight is the realisation that you are the thinker, that you are feeling your thinking, not what is happening around you.

There is no technique you have to apply. No willpower is necessary, because this understanding is innate. It's part of you. As soon as you wake up to the spiritual fact of how life works, you are free. This realisation has the capacity to transform not only your golfing performance and experience, but the way your life unfolds away from the course as well.

'Achieving mental stability [on or off the golf course] is a matter of finding healthy thoughts from moment to moment. Such thoughts can be light years, or a second away.'

—*Syd Banks*

When you see the role Thought plays in creating our experience, life feels easy. There's nothing you need to do. You don't have to force, strive or suffer, accept or surrender, work at it, or remember to do anything. It's the complete opposite of how my life and golf used to feel. It feels free.

There are no strategies I have to apply; no rituals or routines I need to perform. It feels like it was always part of me. Something I have rediscovered after losing touch with it, rather than something I've learned and had to work hard at.

This is the beauty of what I know. Deep down, underneath layers of insecure thinking, there was never anything wrong with me. I was happy and confident as a youngster. I did well in the classroom and on the sports field without knowing how or why, or feeling like I was working hard. I just got on with life and had fun.

Somewhere in my teens I started to believe a story I was telling myself, that in order to be happy and successful I needed to do something more, to be something more than I already was. Many people seem to be labouring under the same misunderstanding, believing a similar made up story. Fortunately, there isn't anything wrong with them either. Once they see it's all made up, they'll be fine.

The Three Principles: Mind, Consciousness and Thought.

Banks describes the three elements of the human psychological experience as 'Mind, Consciousness and Thought.' These words may mean different things to different people. The principles they point to have been experienced and observed in philosophy, science and religion for millennia. In the next three chapters we will see how these elements combine to create our experience of golf, and of life.

'Mind' is the word Syd Banks uses for the formless spiritual energy that lies at the origins of the universe. This universal intelligence connects all living things. It is always there, but isn't a controlling force. A religious person might use the word 'God'. If you're a physicist, you might call it the 'quantum field'. Nature, life source and universal energy are other words used.

Attempting to get your intellect around a concept like 'spiritual intelligence' can seem daunting. If you want to think of spiritual intelligence as intuition, inner wisdom or common sense, go ahead. The words don't matter nearly as much as the feeling behind the words.

The intellect finds the concept of spiritual intelligence difficult to grasp. You feel it, rather than think it. If you've ever been in love you know what it feels like. If you have ever stood in nature and noticed your thinking subside to nothing you have felt it. When you stand over a long putt, and you absolutely know beyond any doubt you are going to hole it, you are connected to this intelligence. You are completely present, at one with where you are and what you are doing. The putt often drops.

'Consciousness' allows us to perceive the world via our thoughts. The higher our level of consciousness the clearer our perceptions. When you have awareness for every inch, every fraction of a second of your golf swing, you trust everything happening within that time and

space, you find yourself in the most enjoyable, most productive state of consciousness a golfer can be in. You have found the zone.

'Thought' is the creative force that forms our perception of reality from one moment to the next. Thought is not reality, but it's via thought that our personal reality is formed. Once we understand that our perception of what we think of as 'real' is actually created by our own thinking, we don't have to accept the thinking that it's our golf is making us feel stressed or anxious, or that a particular situation can make us feel more 'under pressure' than another.

We are free to choose whatever meaning we want for the game, and interpret the results of our actions in a way that gives us the most enjoyment. Like Ian Poulter, we too can play the shot, rather than the situation.

How The 'Outside In' Illusion is Created.

The way this illusion works is amazing, but subtle. It's perhaps the main reason human beings are the most successful species on the planet. Our entire reality is created by our thoughts. We can imagine and experience pretty much anything as if it were real. It's like having the best special effects department or virtual reality machine in the world in your own mind.

Thankfully, I don't have scary dreams very often. The last one was a few years ago. I was being chased round my house by a chainsaw wielding zombie. I experienced all the mental and physical symptoms of such a terrifying ordeal as if it were actually happening.

I had the beating heart, heavy breathing, perspiration, tension in my stomach, all the physical manifestations of being scared out of my mind. I remember the combination of relief and exhaustion when I woke up and realised it was just a dream, a convincing illusion created for me using the awesome power of thought.

Dreams are a good example of how we create our reality with our thoughts. They give us a regular insight into how our minds work, but very rarely do we see their significance. In a dream, we create a situation or scenario with our thinking, and in a semi conscious state, experience it as if it were real.

Unfortunately, as with our waking thoughts, we pay more attention to the content of our dreams, what's happening to us, rather than questioning the process of how such a vivid, realistic experience can happen when we are sleeping.

Imagine you had never seen a television set before. You come down the stairs one morning and to your surprise, there's one in your sitting room. It's showing a Tom and Jerry cartoon. You are curious, so you sit down and watch the screen for a few minutes. When the cartoon finishes, you find yourself spending the rest of the day worrying whether Tom will be OK after being hit in the head with the frying pan.

Somehow the question of how the television came to be in your house, what it was made of, how the pictures got into the box and the nature of the energy that was powering it passes you by.

The truth isn't in the content of our thoughts, either

waking or sleeping. The truth lies in the creative process, in the way we experience those thoughts, and how clearly we see that we are the one creating them.

Reality Isn't What You Think.

'Your eyes aren't just viewers, they are also projectors.'

—*Jim Carrey.*

What you think is your your perception of reality, not reality itself. Your mind works this way all the time, not only when you are dreaming. Information comes in through your senses. The special effects department (Thought) makes up its own version of what is 'out there' based on its best interpretation of the information, and we experience it as 'reality'. We've all had the experience of walking down the street and seeing a good friend walking towards us. We feel happy and excited. We wave and shout 'Hey!' only to realise as we get closer, we're enthusiastically greeting a complete stranger, who seems rather surprised.

Our special effects department had taken the reflected waves of light coming in through our eyes and created a 'perception' of our friend. We took that perception as 'real', felt excited and pleased and acted accordingly by waving and greeting them. The thing was, it was never our friend, just our thinking making us believe it was.

Our thinking *always* looks real to us. That's how we're designed to work. We get all of the feelings and physical reactions associated with what our thinking has created for us. If you're feeling hungry, think about your favourite meal. The food isn't there, it's just an image in your mind. You can't actually see it or smell it, but your tummy will start to rumble and your saliva glands wake up at the thought of that first delicious mouthful. Our perceptions of everything we experience as real are created from the Inside Out, not from the Outside In.

Being Fooled by Your Thinking is Inevitable.

Seeing your thinking as real is part of the human experience. We forget we are thinking the thought. We get caught up in the story and forget we are the ones writing it. The golf course seems to be the place where I get fooled most regularly.

When I get anxious or nervous, I don't see it's me thinking insecure thoughts, I just feel the feelings. If I really saw it was me making up a story about what the round or the shot meant, I wouldn't be getting uncomfortable. Those feelings are always telling me the truth, but it's so easy to misunderstand where they are coming from, and what they are trying to tell me.

Our thinking is meant to look real. If it didn't we couldn't be as amazing and creative as we are. We are limited only by the extent of our imaginations. To help guide us, we have a sophisticated early warning system that let us know when we're not seeing the role of thought, and to look more deeply.

Anxious Feelings are Friend, not Foe.

Insecure feelings are telling us something important. They occur to help us navigate through life. I spent much of my golfing life fighting against stress and anxiety. I hated those feelings and wanted to be rid of them. The more I fought and resisted, the worse I felt. I didn't understand what they were actually telling me. I just wanted to stop feeling scared.

Imagine you buy a new car. You're driving along when a dashboard light in the shape of a thermometer comes on. You assume the light means that the engine is overheating, so you pull over. You wait a few minutes and the light goes off, so you press on, only for it to come on again a few miles up the road. This continues for the whole journey and becomes very frustrating.

When you get home you look in the operating manual for the car. You find that somewhat surprisingly, the light comes on when the car gets up to the correct operating temperature, and turns red if the engine gets too hot. The light was giving you the correct information, it was your interpretation of it which was causing you to think there was a problem.

For years it looked to me that my world and the game of golf was making me feel bad. It was unsympathetic to how I thought it should be. I wanted to fight my feelings, to overcome them and to change the circumstances which I thought was causing them.

Now I can see what the fear and anxiety were really telling me. It wasn't the world that needed to change, it was me. More specifically, my perception of the world needed to change. I was seeing the warning light, but coming to the wrong conclusions and taking the wrong actions.

I can see a harsh beauty in the way this system works. The world needs us to wake up and see the connection between what we think and how we feel. Remaining oblivious causes problems for ourselves and therefore for those around us and the wider environment. My own inner wisdom wouldn't let me find peace until I did see it. It kept prodding me till I realised what my insecure feelings were trying to tell me. Unfortunately some people never see it and live in this misunderstanding their whole lives.

As we will discover, we are spiritually and materially connected to everything else around us. We are either unconscious and part of the problems we all face, or we wake up and become part of the solution. The catalyst is realising the connection between our thoughts and how we feel. We have to understand that the way we feel affects the way we behave, and that our behaviour affects ourselves and everyone and everything that we share the planet with. Responsibility for our own mental health starts and ends with us.

What You are Thinking About Isn't the Problem.

Uneasy feelings come from the fact that you are thinking, not necessarily what you are thinking about. As we saw with our dreams, an easy mistake to make when you first start to learn about this understanding is to look at the content of your thinking to explain your state of mind.

Most fields of psychology have been making this innocent error for the past 150 years. Analysing the content of your thoughts leads to – guess what – more thinking.

What you are thinking about isn't important once you realise you made it up. All your feelings are telling you to do is to look inside, to the fact you are thinking, and to let those thoughts pass through. You're free the moment you see that you are the thinker, and that you created the thought.

Trying to think positive thoughts doesn't help. The issue isn't that what you are thinking is 'negative'. The issue is that you are thinking and not realising it. The fact you feel frustrated or cross about a negative appraisal of a situation is bad enough. Analysing your thoughts to see how you can think more positively will make you feel worse as your thinking winds up.

When you see what created the thinking in the first place, your mind will start to clear and more positive thoughts will naturally flow in to replace the negative ones. Which feels better, when you have a lot of repetitive thinking going on, or when your mind is free and clear?

While we're on the subject of judging our thoughts, this is a good time to remember our thinking is just our perception. We've made the judgement based on a made up story about what it means. Our perception of our circumstances may be positive or negative, never the circumstances themselves. The situation is always neutral. Our thoughts can make the circumstances seem either positive or negative.

'Why then 'tis none to you; for there is nothing either good or bad, but thinking makes it so. To me it is a prison.'

—William Shakespeare. Hamlet.

A sobering example is the story of a businessman stuck in traffic on the way to the airport. He becomes more frustrated as he realises he's going to miss his flight. He is on his way to an important meeting, and it looks like a big problem for him and his company. His mind races as all the possible scenarios play out. He is angry at the traffic, angry at himself for not leaving more time, and angry at the world.

He eventually gets to the airport to find the whole place in turmoil. Police and emergency vehicles are blocking the roads, turning people away. Tragically, the plane he was booked on has crashed a few minutes into the flight. There were no survivors.

The traffic he was cursing at an hour ago saved his life.

The truth is, we have no idea how things are meant to turn out. By judging every thought or situation as good or bad, in the light of our expectations, we are just creating stress for ourselves and limiting the possibilities that life might have in store for us. A mind full of worry doesn't leave room for alternative points of view. This has implications when we set rigid goals for our lives. We miss opportunities when our focus is too narrow.

The Mind has a Self-Healing System.

You can't clear your mind by trying to clear it. You know

this if you've ever tried not to think about missing a short putt. When you see it's just your thinking, the thoughts will flow on. We sometimes call this the 'psychological immune system'. The moment you notice insecure feelings telling you something is wrong, the course of action is very simple. Let the thought pass by. You don't need to do anything at all. It's a non action. The anxiety will fade away as your awareness brings you into the present moment. In a few minutes, you can't even remember what you were worrying about.

Your physical body, your skin, flesh and bone has an automatic healing system. It's miraculous when you think about it, but we all take it for granted. If you cut your finger, as long as the wound stays clean, an amazing thing happens. Within a few days, the blood and cells will remove any impurities, knit the flesh back together, new skin will grow over the wound and your finger will heal.

Is it so hard to imagine our psychology might have a similar healing system in place? It works this way for the body. Why would it not work for the mind? Try it. When you notice yourself feeling a little off, feeling a little insecure, just be aware that it's you thinking the thought and your mind will clear. Trying to fix something which is perfectly capable of fixing itself usually makes things worse.

You Perform at Your Best When Your Mind is Clear.

Our level of consciousness fluctuates with our thinking. When your mind is clear and your awareness is high, you have less thinking going on. You start to notice details about what you are doing You get absorbed in the present moment. You feel calm, relaxed, focused and confident. Outstanding performance is more likely, as is effortless learning, swift improvement and high levels of enjoyment.

Many of us have felt at some point that we just know we are going to hole the chip shot we are standing over, or going to hit a tee shot exactly as the circumstances require. The feeling is almost mystical, like we've been here before and seen it happen. We make the stroke and the ball tracks to the hole and falls in as we knew it would. This is our spiritual intelligence, our inner wisdom at work. It feels free and effortless. We just see the shot and let it go.

Usually at this point our intellect kicks in. We start thinking about how we achieved this level of consciousness and how we can repeat it. Of course we can't. The moment is gone, and the harder we try to reach this state again, the further we get from the real reason we achieved it in the first place. We ascend to this level of consciousness because we let our mind clear and our innate abilities take over.

You Don't Need to Have a Clear Mind to Play Well.

Paradoxically, a cluttered mind is no problem as soon as you notice your thoughts are the source of anxious or pressured feelings. You may not feel great, but you will feel free to play on. As Garret Kramer says, 'just stay in the game'. The feelings will subside in their own time.

It's a myth that high level performers are always feeling calm, composed and confident.

There are examples throughout golf history of outstanding performances when circumstances have appeared to be against a player and emotions were running high. The difference is that the great golfers know better than to try to correct those feelings. They let them be and just played on.

A recent example is Rory McIlroy winning the 2014 BMW PGA Championship after breaking off his engagement to tennis player Caroline Wozniaki on the eve of the tournament. Ben Crenshaw won the 1995 US Masters following the death of his mentor and friend Harvey Penick. We can only imagine the thoughts and feelings they had coursing inside them. Somehow, they rose above them, found a connection to the inner space where great performance originates, and found a way to let that performance emerge.

This book is not about helping golfers attain a certain state of mind in order to play well. We can play well regardless of state of mind once we understand where our experience is coming from.

We All Work The Same Way.

Many of us have concerns about what other golfers think about our swing, our shots and our scores. Ask yourself a question. Do you worry more about your own golf, or about what someone else is doing?

In our insecure moments, we believe what other people are thinking about us matters. Once I realised my own thoughts were all made up, it was a small step to realising that what other golfers thought about me was made up too. The worries I had about looking good and being judged by my peers just didn't make sense any more.

Golf is an individual sport rather than a team endeavour, but human relationships are unavoidable and important. A successful golfer will benefit from good relationships with family, friends, coaches, their caddy, sponsors, fellow competitors and fans. Knowing where your feelings originate smooths your interactions with other people.

When you see that feelings come from thought, you realise everyone else's mind works in the same way. If someone does something thoughtless or inconsiderate, you'll realise they are just caught up in their thinking, the same way as you are sometimes. You can let it pass, rather than reacting to their behaviour, getting caught up in your own thoughts, escalating the situation and making it worse.

It might help if you can wait till the person has settled down and then ask them about what they said or did. Calmly point out to them what happened and how it looked to you. You might want to explain how thinking and feelings are connected, rather than talking directly about what happened. It's usually better if you don't make the situation personal.

The more that people around you see this understanding, the more pleasant and productive the environment will be for everyone.

'You Have two Choices. Love or fear.'

—Jim Carrey

When I start talking about love in relation to sport, people sometimes feel a bit confused, maybe uncomfortable. After all, what has love got to do with golf?

Yet when I ask someone why they play golf, they often answer:

'I don't know, I just love it'.

Instinctively we sense that love is at the heart of everything when we enjoy it and perform well. Lots of golfers know they don't play the game to a particularly high standard, but still say they love their golf. You don't need reasons why you love something. Love isn't rational or logical. You don't think it. You feel it. Love doesn't come from the intellectual part of our psyche. Love comes from wisdom, from the spiritual intelligence behind all of life. It comes from the place before thinking, it comes from the soul.

Love is the only feeling that doesn't come directly from thought. We feel love when we get quiet and we connect deeply with the person we're with. If we're alone, maybe out in nature, we get quiet and feel a love for life. We feel the connection to the source, from where we came. When you deeply love something or someone, the feeling is impossible to put into words. It's formless and cannot really be described.

Love is our default state, the 'factory setting' for human beings. It comes before thought. I was doubtful when I questioned Garret about this,

'Hang on, you've spent the past three years telling me

that 100% of what I feel comes from my thinking, no exceptions, and now you're telling me there is an exception?'

Garret's answer was simple. 'Love is what we're made of.' The spiritual intelligence behind life, is love. Young children are a perfect example. They are walking, talking expressions of love. They haven't had to learn to love. They don't apply love as a technique. They don't have to remember to show love. It's what they are and what they do.

Occasionally their thinking gets in the way and they get upset or angry. Children don't get stuck on a thought or in a bad mood. They let it pass and return to love more quickly than adults tend to do.

When you feel anxious or fearful, you are feeling your thinking. You have a choice between listening to your intellect or listening to your inner wisdom. How do you know whether you are hearing your intellect or your common sense? It's tricky, especially when your consciousness is low, thoughts are coming thick and fast and you are reacting to events or circumstances.

I've found the key is slowing down, becoming aware of my thoughts, and listening to where those thoughts are coming from. Intellectual thought feels uncertain, doubtful, anxious or excited and the voice can be loud.

Love, wisdom, common sense or gut instinct always feel right, but it often whispers.

New Understanding, New Game.

Like many misunderstandings and illusions from the

past, the illusion that your feelings are coming from circumstances isn't obvious. Then suddenly, you see that in between an event and a feeling, there is a thought. The world changes in that moment. You detach from the situation and from your thinking about it.

Someday, the illusion that a golf tournament, a bad shot, or a double bogey can cause us to feel anxious, angry, frustrated, will be regarded in the same way as the illusion that the earth is flat. Recognising the role of thought in that illusion can help all golfers to understand why they play, and help them find what they really want from their game.

In the following chapters I will explain how deepening our understanding can help us play without fear, learn and improve faster, and enjoy the game more than ever.

CHAPTER 5

Creating the World From Inside Out.

"Thought creates the world, then says, 'I didn't do it."

—*David Bohm.*

IN THE PREVIOUS CHAPTER I outlined how the three psychological principles of Mind, Consciousness and Thought combine to create our experience of life. They allow us to be aware of that experience, and to tap into a wisdom much deeper than our own intellectual knowledge. Seeing these principles led to a complete change in how I felt when I played golf. I went from feeling anxious and insecure most of the time, to barely noticing how I was feeling, a sure sign that things had changed for me.

In this chapter, I will explain in more detail how we use Thought to create our world. Understanding the way our thinking affects our moods, feelings and behaviour is a significant leverage point for improving the way we play, learn and experience the game.

Syd Banks describes Thought as 'The Missing Link' because of the way it is hidden in plain sight. We have moments when we are aware we are thinking, but much of the time we don't realise. In a low state of mind we don't see that we are the one thinking our thoughts. Something happens, for example our ball goes out of bounds. We feel an emotion, probably frustration or anger, and it looks to us like our feelings are coming directly from that event.

What we don't see is that in between the event and the feeling, there is thought. This is the missing link. It is only when we realise that we are the thinker and are creating our own perception of what just happened, do we have a choice about how we feel about the event, and our reaction to it. We have limited control over the circumstances we find ourselves in. The event is in the past so we can't change it.

How Thought Works.

Everything created or achieved by human beings started with a thought. From the wheel, the jet engine, the internet, climbing Everest, discovering penicillin, landing on the moon, the Ping Anser putter, to the titanium driver and the laptop I'm typing these words on, a human being had to have a thought for the object to come into existence or the event to occur. They took form in someone's imagination. The thought looked real to that person, the concept made sense to them and they acted to bring that thought from the formless into being.

You use this process every time you make a swing. Every shot you hit starts as a thought in your mind, perhaps as a visualisation of what you want the shot to look like. That thought may lead to a feeling, a sensation in your body of how the swing will develop. You act on that thought. You bring it to form, into reality, by selecting a club and going through the process of swinging and hitting the ball.

The shot may or may not work out the way you intended. That's the game. The important thing to see is that you created something out of nothing. It all started in your mind via Thought.

Unfortunately, the 'creative' process initiated by Thought can also be destructive. The nuclear attack on Hiroshima, the Holocaust, high school shootings and suicide bombings all came about via the same process in a human mind.

I'm writing this chapter the week after the terrible gun attacks on Paris in November 2015. Despite the speculation on the causes behind these outrages, the chain of events is terrifyingly simple. A human being in a low state of consciousness had a thought which made sense to him in that state. He chose to act on that thought with horrific consequences.

Free will is arguably the finest gift we have as human beings. The ultimate proof of this freedom is our ability to choose which thoughts we act upon, and which we let pass. Greek philosopher Aristotle said;

'It is the mark of an educated mind to be able to entertain a thought without accepting it.'

By understanding the thought process, and seeing that our feelings come from what we think about, we see that we have a choice. We can't choose our thoughts, but we can choose to what extent we let those thoughts influence our actions and behaviour. We can choose what we accept from our flow of thinking, and what we don't. We always have a choice how we respond to our experience of our environment, even though we may not realise it at the time.

There is a spectrum of how clearly we see our freedom of will. When we are in a high state of consciousness, when our mind is clear, we see that we are the thinker. We let insecure thoughts pass without paying much attention to them. At the other end of the spectrum, when our state of mind is low, we are caught up in our thoughts. We forget that we are the one thinking them. Our insecure thinking looks like 'real life' and it looks troubling. We feel upset or insecure and we want to do something about the situation or circumstance to which we attribute the feeling.

As individuals, our state of mind fluctuates from moment to moment. You're probably aware of this. Our position on this fluctuating spectrum determines how we see the world and how we feel. We will look at the principle of Consciousness in the next Chapter.

Our thinking is designed to work very much behind the scenes, like the special effects department at a film studio. We see or feel the results of our thinking, rarely the thinking itself. The way we see a situation, what we see as 'reality', is actually a perception created by our thoughts.

The moment we see we created that perception, we have a choice about how we feel about it. We can be free from the idea that our golf is making us feel stressed or anxious, or that one situation can make us feel more 'under pressure' than another. The physical and psychological symptoms we feel are real enough, but the process through which we feel them is hidden.

Missing the role of thought in how we feel about things can lead us to blame our job, our relationship, or our golf for our state of mind. The belief that something outside you can and does affect how you feel is the opposite of free will. Your will would not be free if outside circumstances really could affect it.

How does understanding this process allow us to experience more freedom and peace of mind on the golf course, instead of feeling doubt and frustration and worrying when it's all going to go wrong?

Firstly, realise that you are the thinker. You can't control your thoughts, but they're all created by you. You create them and you can choose how you respond to them. You can pay attention to them and let them affect how you feel, or you can let them flow past. Thoughts are just a condensing of mental energy. They are like smoke. Ephemeral, ethereal, you can't control them any more than you can control the weather. Thoughts will come in whether you like it or not, but you can choose which ones you energise and which ones you allow to pass.

A thought comes into our consciousness. Our feelings can change before we even have a chance to recognise precisely what the thought was or where it came from. It is so misleading when a coach or psychologist tells us to control what we think about, or to control our emotions. Good luck if you believe you can control the chain reaction that leads from thought to feeling! We see the ball land in the water and the feelings of frustration and disappointment are upon us.

What gives thought power, or gives us power over thought, is what we do next. If we realise we are the thinker, we understand where the feelings came from and have some control over how we respond, rather than being a victim of our situation. We can stay attached to our angry thoughts and let them influence what we do next, or we can allow our thinking to move on to the next shot.

Let's recap on what we learned about the nature of Thought from Chapter Four.

- Our feelings come from our thinking, not from the situation or circumstances.
- What you think of as reality isn't reality. It's just your perception of reality.
- Perennially misunderstanding points one and two is inevitable. It's part of being human.
- Humans have a psychological immune system. When thinking subsides, clarity returns and how we feel improves. This happens naturally without any conscious or deliberate actions from us.
- Humans tend to learn and perform better when they have less thinking going on, rather than more.

Thought is 'Content Neutral'.

'The Inner Game of Golf' by Tim Gallwey is one of the

most significant golf books of the last fifty years. Gallwey was among the first to focus on the psychological aspects of the game. With millions of copies sold, it remains on the bookshelves of serious and not so serious golfers alike.

The book explores the a number of different areas of the game, from learning, to performance, to practice, to dealing with 'pressure'. The parts of the book that deal with awareness and how we learn new movement are excellent. However, Gallwey makes the mistake of analysing the content of our thinking, as we all do from time to time.

To me, the voice in our heads he describes as 'Self 1' is Thought. The quiet, powerful, capable entity he calls 'Self 2' is our inner wisdom, the silent space within us from where our best golf originates. This psychological space before the contamination of thought is 'Mind'. Gallwey is describing the same psychological principles as Syd Banks, but using different language.

Large sections of The Inner Game of Golf are devoted to analysing what 'Self 1' (our thinking) is saying, and how we should deal with it. Unfortunately, this is where Gallwey gets off track. Analysing the content of our thoughts is largely a waste of mental energy. I spent years doing this and it didn't make me feel or play any better. Thought is just thought, mental energy manifesting as chatter. It flows into our awareness and flows out again like driftwood floating down a river.

If you understand how your mind works, you don't need to analyse or interpret thoughts. You just let them flow. Devoting mental energy to analysing your thinking, gives credence to the myth that all thought is important, that every thought we have means something and warrants attention. When you analyse thought, you give energy and attention to something which on its own is neutral and powerless. You create a cycle of thinking.

Gallwey's assessment that thinking (Self 1) interferes with our natural ability to perform with effortless excellence is correct. He has the right diagnosis, but then heads off up a blind alley by suggesting a number of techniques to 'keep Self 1 quiet' and stop thought interfering with our natural instincts (Self 2). Such techniques may work in the short term, but are counter-productive. The additional thinking that comes with implementing techniques and strategies will make things worse not better.

There are moments in the book where I believe Gallwey sees the truth. On page 43 he says:

'Dealing effectively with these mental obstacles need not involve deep introspection or self-analysis. Golfers don't need to lie on the couch or repent their sins.'

I'd go further. Golfers should avoid 'deep introspection and self analysis' at all costs. Unfortunately, Gallwey ignores his own advice. He devotes a whole chapter to analysing the feeling of 'self doubt', and offers strategies for overcoming it.

I agree self-doubt is troublesome since it can lead to over-tightness. Tension is responsible for fluctuations in timing and bad golf shots. However, feelings of self-doubt don't deserve any more attention than other feelings we have. Self-doubt is merely a result of insecure thinking. Left alone, both will pass.

Gallwey is also on the right track when he states:

'The first step is to acknowledge that we are not born into self-doubt. It's hard to find a young child who doesn't believe in himself. Children may trip and fall when learning to walk, or the castle they are building may topple with a misplaced block, but such occurrences are not yet occasions for questioning oneself.'

Young children are confident and rest in their inner wisdom most of the time. This state of mind may stem from the fact a child's intellect isn't fully developed yet and they haven't learnt to over think and second guess themselves. Children allow troubled thinking to pass, and quickly revert back to clarity. They demonstrate resilience and a lack of self doubt we can all learn from.

Left alone, our doubtful thinking will also pass and so will the feelings of self-doubt. By labelling doubtful thinking as a 'problem', we are giving it a significance it otherwise wouldn't have. When we employ techniques to cope with feelings of self-doubt or lack of confidence, we actually make these feelings worse. We stimulate more thinking and the cycle perpetuates.

Timing is Everything.

'Rhythm and timing are the two things which we all must have, yet no one knows how to teach either'.

—*Bobby Jones*

Bobby Jones was the first golfing superstar, probably the finest amateur player of all time. From age twenty one to twenty eight when he retired, Jones played in twenty one majors (the U.S. and British Amateurs counted as majors in Jones's day). He finished first or second seventeen times. He played in eight US Opens and three Open Championships, winning seven and finishing second three times. He won all three Open Championships he competed in during that period.

Jones was a fine golfer, and an astute one. Timing is one of the most important and most overlooked elements of the golf swing. The golf club is swung on an arc. The clubface rotates around the axis of the shaft in relation to that arc. Small errors in timing have dramatic effects on the strike and the flight of the golf ball.

The sequencing has to be precise. It's a miracle good golfers hit the ball so consistently. When a good golfer hits a bad shot, the error is more likely to be a timing error than faulty technique. Golfers with unconventional technique but great rhythm have won major championships. Golfers with technically sound golf swings but inconsistent timing don't win the monthly medal very often.

Timing is the way the parts of the body move in relation to each other, and the way they respond to the swinging of the club. A swing has rhythm and timing. A hit doesn't. The timing of your swing is something you feel, rather than think through step by step. Our feel for the swing depends on our levels of awareness. When thinking slows and the mind clears, awareness is elevated. Therefore, our ability to feel timing, this crucial element of the swing, depends on our levels of thinking. Less thinking allows more awareness, giving greater feel.

I'm coming down the last few holes of a tournament with a lead. My mind wanders on to how nice it would be to win, what I'm going to say in my winner's speech, maybe how I'm going to spend the money. These thoughts are completely natural and normal. I can try to resist them in the same way that I could resist waves running up onto the beach. As my thinking flows onto what I need to do to close the tournament out I start to get some anxious feelings. I might feel a tightness in my gut, and my hands and arms might feel weak and shaky.

Sports psychologists told me the thoughts that caused these feelings were bad or negative. They advised me not to think them, that I should 'stay in the present'. This advice wasn't much help. I can't 'unthink' what I just thought. I can't control what thoughts come into my head and when.

I have thousands of thoughts a day, most of which are random, a few of which I wouldn't want to share. I'd be in prison or six feet under if I acted on some of the thoughts I've had over the years. All thoughts are neutral. In trying to replace a bad thought with a better one, a 'positive thought', I'm stimulating more thinking. This prevents my mind from returning to clarity and to awareness.

Rather than listening to the psychologists, if I get quiet, I might be able to sense where the thinking is coming from. I might hear my own inner wisdom. I might simply notice: 'It's OK, I've got some thinking happening here.' If I'm absorbed in the process of playing the next shot, I might just get the sense that there's something going on in the background, a bit like a TV elsewhere in the house showing a programme I'm not really interested in. My mind settles back to calmness and clarity.

I now understand that if a thought brings an anxious, excited or uncomfortable feeling, it's a warning. A signal from my inner wisdom to tell me I've forgotten I'm the one thinking the thoughts, that I'm the one making up the story. If I heed the warning I'll choose to let the thoughts flow by and just keep playing.

The anxious reaction started by an overactive intellect appears to be the result of the situation we find ourselves in. It's natural to react in these situations, to think harder about how to change our circumstances and alleviate our unease. As we now know, our feelings stem from our thoughts. Our thoughts are a representation of the situation which our 'special effects department' has created. Our feelings don't stem from a particular circumstance. One day we feel uncomfortable coming down the last few holes, the next day we play the same stretch without a care in the world.

For years I misread my anxious feelings. I thought they were telling me that the situation was making me feel bad. I set out to play golf, a game I played for fun. Yet often I felt like I was walking through a minefield. Other than pick my ball up and head back to the club-house, my options for changing my circumstances were limited.

So I reached for a coping technique, positive thinking, deep breathing, a routine – something to try to mitigate my anxiety. Evaluating my thinking added more thought to an already overloaded system. The tight, anxious feelings got worse rather than better. It was hard to play well in this state because the tension played havoc with my golf swing. My timing and feel were severely impaired, especially on short shots and putts.

Now when I have a chance to win, my state of mind is different. I can take the warning signals as a welcome reminder that I have some thinking going on. My job is to keep playing. The psychological immune system will kick in, thought will flow and fearful feelings will dissipate. I fully acknowledge this is easier said than done in the heat of the moment. The insight was the realisation that I am thinking the thoughts and a connection to the place my thinking is coming from. Now I see separation between events and what I'm feeling.

The moment a golfer understands pressure doesn't emanate from the tournament, the scorecard or from competitors, but from their own thinking, feelings can change in an instant. I'll consider this book a success if that is the only thing you take from it.

Overcoming the fear and anxiety I used to feel during a round of golf is the most important benefit from understanding the connection between my thoughts and my state of mind. The tightness I sometimes feel during a round eases more quickly. My rhythm is better. My ball striking has become more reliable as a result of allowing insecure 'how to do it' thinking to pass by.

Swing Thoughts or Swing Feelings?

Our ability to feel the timing of a golf swing is dependent on our levels of awareness. More awareness, better timing. Our awareness, our level of consciousness, depends on the amount of thinking we engage in. More thinking, less awareness.

I'm not a big fan of predetermined, conscious 'swing thoughts'. Many times I've played well with a particular swing thought and said to myself: 'That's it, I've got it!' – only to find it doesn't have the same effect, or give me the same feeling in my swing the next day. I would try to work out what was different, why it didn't feel the same, or I would panic and start searching for thought that did work.

I couldn't imagine playing an important round without a thought to control my swing. 'I can't not think of anything!' Again, I was misguided. I believed that my golf swing worked better when I managed and controlled it with my intellect rather than allowing my innate ability and natural talent to do what I knew they could do.

It's easy to believe intellectual thought is essential to perform the golf swing correctly. We learn by thinking how to swing, attempting what we thought about, evaluating the results and making changes based on that evaluation. This process works for a while, before our thinking recedes into the background and the movement becomes instinctive.

If a certain swing thought coincides with you playing well, if you believe that thought was the reason for success, you will be tempted to hang onto that swing thought the next time you play. Unfortunately our thoughts aren't meant to hang around. They flow through our consciousness like water flowing under a bridge. When we get stuck on a thought, it clogs up the system and we start to feel bound up and uneasy. Performing to our potential is less likely as our level of consciousness drops.

Thoughts come and go. We jam the system by trying to prescribe or manage the natural ebb and flow of our thinking. Our heads fill with old, stale ideas, leaving no room for insights, fresh thinking to flow in. Our instincts and intuition are the true source of good decision making and creative play. Our instincts thrive when we look towards awareness and away from prescribed thoughts or mental strategies.

We stifle awareness of what we are actually doing and feeling in the moment when we have a list of key swing thoughts. We become obsessed with what we think we should be doing. When awareness is high we have no agenda, no expectations. We feel free and play the shot in front of us. We absorb the information coming through our senses, respond instinctively and our actions are highly appropriate.

You're a Golfer, Not a Robot.

By now you might be thinking, like I did for a while, that thinking is bad, that it's the cause of our problems. Not true. The principle of Thought is neutral. Syd Banks describes it as 'a spiritual tool' and, like any tool, it can be used in a number of ways. Remember, thought is our special effects department. It's capable of creating any experience we can imagine. Every great shot we hit begins life as a thought. We are at our best when we are at our most creative.

Playing 'golf swing' or trying to repeat a swing, feels stifling and clunky because it reduces us from being creative, free thinking athletes, to being robots. Our intellect says that if we follow a set of instructions – stand like this, then do this, then this, then this – the perfect golf shot will always result. Unfortunately this isn't the case, partly because as we will see later, we don't always do what we think we are doing.

We play our best golf when we approach the ball with an elevated awareness of our surroundings, ourselves and the task at hand. The perfect shot for the situation comes to us. We step up to the ball with confidence and the shot we have 'seen' in our minds eye happens. We play our best golf when we are free and creative, playing intuitively, not when we are trying to be golfing machines.

I believe many golfers struggle with short putts because it's hard to see a straight three footer as an opportunity to be creative. Somehow a recovery shot out of the forest is less mentally taxing, because it calls for maximum creativity. The awesome power of our imagination takes over and we become absorbed in the process. Often we don't even know how we hit the shot. The ball sails up through the gap in the trees, curves to the left and lands on the middle of the green. It's almost like someone else did it.

It can be hard to see short putts or easy chips as a chance to create something. We think of them as shots we mustn't mess up. Consequently, we dwell on the mechanics of the stroke, become robotic and try to ensure we don't. The result is anxiety and tension over such shots rather than relaxation and concentration.

The best putters always seem very artistic to me, whether it's over a four footer or a forty footer. Some great putters of the past have talked about hooking or slicing short putts into the slope depending on the break. I'm not advocating you copy this approach. Just become more aware of your thinking on holing out or short chip shots. Are you creating a beautiful little golf shot, or trying not to make a mistake? The answer will be found in how you feel.

Practising or Warming Up?

The chance to hit balls before we play is a bonus for most golfers. The norm is to rush onto the tee on a Saturday morning with a bacon sandwich and a takeaway coffee rather than warming up the muscles and settling into a nice calm frame of mind. Unfortunately, most golfers (myself included on occasion) 'warm up' in a way which isn't helpful. It's something to watch out for if you rarely practice other than before you play.

The temptation is to turn the warm up into a practice session, to start thinking about how to improve your swing. Instead of warming up your muscles, you try to swing the club 'properly', put into practice what you worked on in your last lesson or try some key swing thoughts. This mini-practice session doesn't improve awareness. Nor does it free up the body to swing naturally. We fill our heads with unnecessary thinking, rather than clear our minds and warm our muscles in preparation to play instinctive, free flowing golf.

I find it more helpful to loosen up with an open mind, instead of preconceived thoughts. I start swinging, hitting a few wedges. My sole focus is to be aware of what I'm doing. I'm 'listening' for a feeling, sensing whether any part of my swing or part of my body feels different, or whether I'm drawn to a particular movement or sensation.

What I'm feeling as I swing may or may not be something I've felt before, but something will come to my attention before too long. When that happens, I just go with the flow. It might be rhythm, it might be the way a particular part of my body is moving or feeling. It might be a sense of balance or stability. Whatever seems important in my warm-up session becomes my awareness for the day. I'll stick with it for as long as it feels right. Sometimes the whole round, sometimes I become aware of something else and go with that instead. I'm feeling what I'm doing and trusting my instincts, rather than thinking and getting stuck.

The Score, The Results and The Consequences.

When you begin to see how overthinking interferes with your natural ability to play the game, you might conclude that I'm advocating a detached, indifferent approach, that wandering around listening to the birds and smelling the flowers without caring about your golf is the route to enjoyment and success. I tried this for a while. I tried to be totally detached whenever I stepped onto a golf course. I thought maybe I was getting anxious because I was taking golf too seriously. Maybe caring less could be the answer?

As with all innocent attempts to manage my thinking, this was a trap. Thinking 'I don't care any more' became a strategy to cope with the thoughts and feelings I believed were hampering my performance. However, pretending I didn't care just made me feel I wasn't giving my best effort, that I wasn't bothered, that I wasn't doing myself or the game justice. Consequently, my enthusiasm and enjoyment diminished. I knew I wasn't being honest with myself and as you can imagine, my results weren't good.

Like most golfers, I'm naturally competitive. I love to play tournaments. I love a hard fought game with my friends at Woburn. There's usually a few quid riding on the outcome. I love to win and I hate losing. I really enjoy the bragging and banter afterwards.

It's easy to forget that the feeling of excitement from winning or disappointment of a loss is just something I've created with my thinking. I'm free to feel all of those things and experience them for their own sake, rather than making up a story about what it all means in the rest of my life. I know where my feelings come from. I know my life isn't really going to change whether I win or lose. I can play full out and fearlessly, knowing whatever happens, I'm going to be fine when the game is done.

To me, this is the true meaning of mental strength, of inner resilience.

Betting and wagering has probably been a part of golf since shepherds started hitting stones into rabbit holes with their crooks in the 1600s. I know golfers who can't get motivated for a game unless there is some sort of 'interest', a financial stake to make the game more exciting for them.

It is a great example of golfers misunderstanding the nature of thought and how their feelings come to pass. Perhaps more accurately, it shows how we wilfully ignore the fact that our feelings come from the story we have made up about what the game or the shot means. In the cold light of day, we know a bet on the match won't really change how we feel about the outcome. We want to win anyway, we don't like losing.

However, I know millionaires who will happily admit to being a nervous wreck standing over a four foot putt on the final green to win ten pounds from a mate. If this example doesn't prove our feelings come from the story we've made up about what the game means, I'm not sure what does.

I'm one of many golfers who like the excitement, the feeling of having something at risk when they play. Money won on the golf course seems so much sweeter than money earned at work! It's why betting has become such a big part of golf. Of course the element of risk, the jeopardy of losing are all part of a story we have made up.

The beauty of all games is they can mean anything we want them to mean, depending on the thoughts we have about them. If you believe that holing a putt is crucial to the outcome of the story you have made up about the game, that is certainly how it will feel in the moment you are putting it.

Problems arise when we forget it's a game we have ascribed a meaning to, and we allow thoughts about our performance to affect our mood long after the final putt has been sunk. Feeling bad for hours after a bad round is a sign that your thinking is a problem, much more so than your golf swing or putting.

The reason we feel bad is a function of the gap between 'reality' (I'm losing) and the story we are telling ourselves (life will be better if I win). It's the fact we're thinking. The story looks real because we've forgotten we are the story teller. We want to do something about an imaginary situation fabricated by our insecure thinking. This is the first mistake. The second mistake causes more of a problem.

Our warning system sends out some information in the form of anxious feelings. The message is: 'Your thinking is getting a bit off track here.' Unfortunately, we often misinterpret this warning signal. We think it says: "The situation we are in is the cause of these feelings. You need to do something to change that situation!' Now your thinking revs up as you run through possible solutions; change the swing, concentrate, relax – which makes us more agitated and makes the apparent need for action even more urgent.

The more we thrash around piling thinking onto more thinking, the lower our state of mind descends. The mind's natural healing agent, the psychological immune system, has no chance to do its job and the worse we feel. Our level of play descends further. At its most severe, the mind becomes overwhelmed by thought and begins to shut down, perhaps to protect itself.

When this happens during a round, it can result in the yips, or flinches. Some of the world's best players have suffered them from time to time.

Many golfers will feel helpless at this point and give up completely. Ironically, this instinctive surrender and acceptance of the situation creates a gap in the barrage of thought. The mind begins to clear, the anxiety subsides, and a few good shots begin to appear. This more positive state continues for a few holes, until the golfer realises the score is back towards their expectations, at which point the thinking starts again and tension levels rise.

Loving the Game Doesn't Require Thought.

I love golf. When I'm playing with freedom, full awareness and I'm totally present, I feel it more. My enjoyment drops when my thinking gets in the way and my consciousness subsides. I don't feel the same way about the game when I'm believing the made up stories about what it will mean if I hole this putt or shoot this score.

Your feelings are your guide when your thinking is getting in the way. Creativity, trust, and awareness feel very different from insecurity, doubt, anxiety and neediness. By tuning into your feelings, you have an early warning system always keeping you on track and keeping your best interests at heart.

Golf played in this quiet, simple state of mind is the most enjoyable form of the game I know. It's love, pure and simple, golf for golf's sake. This is why we play.

CHAPTER 6

The Gap Between Feel and Real.

'The capacity to be aware and experience life is innate in human beings. It is a universal phenomenon. Our level of awareness in any moment determines the quality of our experience.'

—*Michael Neill. The Inside Out Revolution*

IN THE PREVIOUS CHAPTER, WE looked at the principle of Thought, the psychological tool human beings use to create our perception of the world. We looked at how our 'special effects department' works, and how we can get confused and stressed when we are fooled by the illusion that everything we think is real. This confusion is a frequent occurrence because our thinking is designed to look totally convincing. As quantum physicist David Bohm puts it,

'Thought creates our world, then says, I didn't do it'.

In this chapter, we look at the principle of Consciousness. Our level of consciousness determines the quality of our experience. Awareness is Consciousness in action. Thought projects our perceptions onto the screen that is our awareness.

Our senses – what we see, hear, smell and feel – our receptors for information about our environment, are also part of this creative perceptive process. If we weren't conscious, if we had no awareness, we would have no cognition of what our special effects department was creating. Understanding the consequences of our level of Consciousness in the moment is vital for a golfer. Enjoyment and performance is diminished when our awareness drops. We lose ourselves in thought and we forget we are creating our own story about what is happening in the game.

'Awareness is Curative.'

—Tim Gallwey, The Inner Game of Golf

Gallwey's observation that Awareness is the most important factor in learning and playing the game, has the potential to fundamentally change how golf is played and experienced. He suggests the way many golfers attempt to learn the game is flawed and makes progress much harder than it should be.

His frustrations with golf coaching are as relevant today as when he wrote about them in the 1970s. Mainstream golf instruction has gone in a more information driven, less instinctive direction. Technology has enabled more analysis, more dissection, more fragmentation and a proliferation of swing models and techniques. Very rarely do we get pointed in the direction of what comes naturally to all of us, what's inside us, to our innate talent and potential. Ball flight and club data, biomechanics and sports science are used to establish theoretical ideals, rather than as feedback to help golfers compare and confirm what they actually feel during a swing.

> 'The Inner Game approach to learning is based on a fundamental and powerful principle of change. I call it the Law of Awareness. In simplest form, this law states that if you want to change something, first increase your awareness of the way it is. Awareness itself is curative.'
>
> —Tim Gallwey. The Inner Game of Golf.

The idea that you can change the behaviour of something just by being aware of it might sound far fetched. However, as any primary school teacher will confirm, the behaviour in the classroom is very different when the children know they are being watched. There is a recognised scientific phenomenon where a similar effect is observed.

> 'German physicist Werner Heisenberg advanced the theory in the 1920s that electrons, one of the particles that make up an atom, do not always exist. They only exist when someone or something observes them or watches them. The theory goes on to say that nothing can exist in the same form when it is observed, compared to when it isn't. Just by being present, by watching and observing, the subject's behaviour will be changed.'
>
> —Carlo Rovelli. Seven Brief Lessons on Physics.

Gallwey devised an exercise called 'Back, Hit.' Most golfers have tried it at some point. You say 'Back' when the club changes direction at the top of the backswing, and 'Hit' when the club strikes the ball. This exercise encourages awareness of where the clubhead actually is during the swing, rather than thinking about where it 'should' be.

Gallwey says:

'I realised, as I had with tennis, that there is a very big difference between observing your swing, and trying to control it. Most important, I found out that it's hard to do both at the same time. When I kept to the discipline of the exercise, paying full attention, I had much less tendency to over control my swing, and as a result, it seemed over time to gain control naturally.'

Most golfers spend considerable time and effort trying to wilfully change parts of their swing. Gallwey suggests that the movement can be altered simply by raising your level of awareness as you swing. Increased consciousness is all you need to enhance both learning and performance.

I have seen compelling evidence for this, both in changing my own golf swing and in helping other golfers change theirs.

The Key to Consistency.

In Chapter Five we explored the nature of thought. We now know our thinking is always in flux. When we block the flow by recycling the same swing thought, it feels unnatural. Our instincts are to allow our thinking to change and flow. Often this thinking revolves around the result of the previous shot. If we react to our thinking, we try to swing differently on every shot. As a result we are always chasing our tail.

This process isn't helpful, but is understandable now we know how thought works. Thought looks real, so it makes sense for golfers to act on what they thought went wrong with the previous shot. It might not work any better than returning to the same swing thought, but it makes more sense to most golfers than repeating the thought that preceded and possibly caused the previous bad shot.

So what do we do? We are between a rock and a hard place. Swinging differently based on our thoughts about the previous swing doesn't work. Neither does keeping the same swing thought for every swing. What should we be thinking about when we are standing over the golf ball? Is it possible not to think about anything at all when we swing?

To many golfers, the difference between thinking and awareness is not immediately obvious. The easiest way to define it is this.

Thinking is in the future or the past; what happened, what might happen, what you should be doing, what you don't want to be doing.

Awareness is in the present. It is seeing, hearing and feeling what you are actually doing.

There are many benefits of making awareness a priority when practicing, learning and playing.

The first is consistency of mind-set. You can approach every shot in the same way, regardless of whether it is in practice, during a lesson, in a friendly game, the monthly medal, or the last round of the Open Championship. Consistently good results are more likely from a consistently high level of consciousness.

The Space Where Miracles Can Happen.

Anyone who has played the game for more than a few weeks knows the mind and body make all sorts of minute adjustments to swing path, clubface alignment, timing and low point during the swing. We have little awareness of how these adjustments occur, although you may be familiar with the sensation of the hands 'saving' the shot at the last moment. Something wasn't quite right earlier in the swing but you managed to make a correction to get the shot on target.

Our intellect can't really comprehend the way our senses and instincts coordinate the movements to get the shot away, because the intelligence which controls movement is upstream of the intellect.

When you analyse the factors involved, you might conclude that every good golf shot is a minor miracle. The sweet spot on the golf club is roughly the size of a ten pence piece. It moves over forty feet, at a maximum speed of between eighty and 120 miles per hour. The clubface is rotating around the axis of the shaft at around fifteen hundred degrees per second as it approaches impact. The margins for error are measured in milliseconds and fractions of an inch. Time and again a good golfer delivers the clubhead well inside those margins to send the ball soaring to the target.

There is no way a human being can control every variable in the swing by thinking about it, and then acting on those thoughts. Our reaction time is around one third of a second. By the time we have become aware of something in the downswing and consciously tried to change it, the ball is already fifty yards up the fairway.

The way most people use their mind to learn golf could be compared to a computer connected to the internet. The computing power of a single PC is puny compared to the network of processors and storage which make up the world wide web. When we try to swing a golf club using conscious swing thoughts and intellectual understanding we are offline. We work so hard with a small, slow processor, and shut off a source of infinite wisdom and intelligence which is always available to us.

When we raise our awareness, we create a space in the flow of thought where these small miracles, our best golf shots, can happen on a regular basis. Through awareness of what is happening while it's happening, we provide the subconscious with high quality, real time information about the variables in the swing – where the club is in relation to our body, where our balance is, the orientation of the clubface in relation to the ball and the target. Our ability to make small, last millisecond adjustments is enhanced as the quality of information improves.

Our thinking seems to quieten down when the mind is absorbed in awareness of what is happening. It's like a video camera switched to record rather than play. Information flows freely along a clear channel between the senses gathering information and the subconscious mind, to the body swinging the golf club.

Our performance can be amazing when our level of awareness is high and we trust our subconscious capabilities. Often a golfer is lost for words after a particularly good round. When I've played my best golf, it feels like I'm passively observing myself play rather than controlling what was happening. Excellence is happening through me, rather than as a result of my conscious actions.

A golfer can improve their consistency immediately by making awareness the primary focus on every swing. By approaching every shot in the same way, our thinking slows, allowing our Consciousness to rise. Awareness solves the problem of what to think or not to think when we are standing over a golf shot.

This doesn't mean that thinking isn't happening. At a deeper level the impulses which instigate and guide the swing still occur. This level of subconscious control is more than capable of producing results we can be proud of. The only thing intellectual interference will achieve is to prevent good golf from occurring. We will look at how this works in Chapter Eight.

Seeing into the Future.

'Staying in the present' is a well-worn cliché in golf and other sports. It's a phrase often used when a golfer is asked about their approach to an important round of golf. But what exactly is the present? We observe it in relation to what came before, our past, which no longer exists, and our future, which does not yet exist.

Quite simply: The concept of 'the present' is subjective. It's a thought, rather than a something tangible.

Most of us have experienced the feeling of knowing we are going to hole a putt, or pull off a particularly difficult shot. It's one of the most awesome experiences in golf when it happens. It seems we experience an elevated level of consciousness allowing us to see the future before it unfolds. This sounds unlikely, yet we've all done it. It begs the questions, 'How does this occur'? and 'Why can't we do it more often?' To answer these questions, we need to ask another. What exactly is the flow of time, and where exactly are we in that flow?

How do we explain the phenomenon of 'knowing' we are going to hole the putt if we are only ever in the present moment? How can we explain our varying perceptions of the flow of time? Could it be down to our varying levels of awareness from moment to moment?

Ben Hogan is reported to have said when he was playing his best, he felt *'time slowed'* to the extent he could actually see the clubface hitting the ball. I've never got close to that heightened state of consciousness, but I certainly believe it's possible.

The nature of time and our relationship to it has been discussed by scientists and thinkers for centuries.

'Physicists and philosophers have come to the conclusion that the idea of a present that is common to the whole universe is an illusion, and that the universal 'flow' of time is a generalisation which doesn't work.'

—Carlo Rovelli, Seven Brief Lessons on Physics.

Most people have experienced time seeming to speed up or slow down depending on their level of engagement with what they are doing. When we are playing well, we seem to have lots of time. Yet time seems to speed up when things start to go wrong on the golf course. Events run away from us. Conversely, when we are enjoying ourselves time seems to fly by, when we are bored or distracted by our thinking, time drags more slowly.

There are a number of theories about the nature of the flow of time. Scientists point in the general direction of the intersection of gravity, quantum mechanics and thermodynamics, but struggle to be more specific. Maybe we should contemplate the possibility of a spiritual dimension to time, in the same way there's a spiritual dimension to our experience of reality via our thinking?

At elevated states of consciousness, maybe we can experience the past, the future and the present at the same time?

I find it interesting that this phenomenon of 'knowing' we're going to hit a good shot happens infrequently, yet almost every golfer I speak to has experienced it. I've yet to hear an explanation of why or how it happens, or how we can make it happen in the future.

The elusive nature of the experience suggests most of us play golf in a low state of consciousness. Our awareness levels are poor most of the time. As consciousness rises, maybe it will happen more often? Maybe this is a secret the great players keep to themselves?

All of this conjecture points us in the direction of the possible, rather than the proven. As we have seen, we have the power to create our own reality with our thinking. Why not make it a positive, optimistic reality? Optimism is a powerful card for a golfer to have up his sleeve. You can pay attention to the thought which sees a putt stopping six feet short, or the one where it tracks into the middle of the hole.

At low level of Consciousness, you only see the bad putt. At a higher level you realise you have the choice. From the highest level, the thought of missing doesn't even enter your head.

Increasing levels of awareness, both of thought and deed, is one thing most golfers can do without changing anything technically. It would improve their performance in minutes. That isn't to say they won't improve technically. They will. Gallwey's 'law of awareness' will ensure improvement happens effortlessly, without trying hard or grinding.

Learning is Natural.

Tim Gallwey and Fred Shoemaker cite awareness as the most important element in the learning process. I can't disagree. Magical things begin to happen when we become truly aware, rather than guessing at what we're doing. It is crucial we become aware of what we are thinking when we are swinging. All our movements are initiated with a thought, an impulse from the brain to the body. If we aren't aware of our true intentions when we swing, changing a movement pattern becomes difficult.

We need to be aware of what we know, but also of what we don't know. We all have blind spots. We have parts of our golf swing and putting strokes where we don't really know what's happening. Why don't we know? We are the ones gripping the club, swinging it. Yet we often don't have a clue where the club head is in relation to our bodies, the ball or the ground. How can that be?

There is a well known saying in golf coaching, there is often a huge difference between 'Feel', what the golfer thinks they are doing, and 'Real', what they are actually doing. The first step to improving is to close this gap between feel and real.

Blind spots are the hidden enemy. We can't expect to make changes in the way we move if we don't have sufficient awareness to feel, in real time, what our body is actually doing during the swing.

Many golfers are surprised when they see their own golf swings. Mobile phone camera technology has improved so much. Golfers are more familiar with their own golf swing than 30 years ago, when video cameras were expensive, cumbersome and awkward to use.

There is a common response when I film a student during a lesson:

'I had no idea I did that'.

What are golfers aware of when swinging if they aren't feeling what is actually going on? The answer is not very much. They are caught up in the past or the future. Thinking about what they should be doing rather than being aware of what they're actually doing. They think about what they're trying to do, what they're supposed to do, what they mustn't do, what they want or don't want to happen, and what it will mean if it does or doesn't happen.

All this mental clutter, this intellectualisation of the golf swing, doesn't leave much room for awareness of the current moment, for feeling, sensing or being.

Excessive thinking leaves us frustrated, annoyed, anxious and in a low state of consciousness. Our awareness is suppressed. We either go through the motions on autopilot, our senses dulled by layers of insecure thought, or we try too hard, willing our bodies to swing the club in a fashion we have decided is 'correct'.

Get Curious!

So how do we raise our awareness levels so we start to notice and feel what is happening? The easiest way I've found is to get curious about the part of the swing where you have a blind spot. If you can identify the moment where you lose awareness of what the club or a particular part of the body is doing, you have illuminated that blind spot. Consciousness has risen.

Curiosity is a natural human instinct. It is the gateway to raised levels of awareness, consciousness and understanding. You deepen your awareness when you get curious about something. You start to notice things, see things differently, find options and possibilities. Curiosity about a new toy or a new environment is how we learn as children. Curiosity is the gateway to concentration, to absorption, to fascination and to understanding.

As I mentioned earlier, many golfers have a different state of mind in different situations. They struggle to take their best golf from the practice ground to the golf course, and especially into competition. Golfers 'working' on their swings in practice are normally thinking about what they are trying to do. Their mental conversation goes something like:

'First I need to do this, then this, then this... and that will lead to a good shot.'

The golf swing happens in less than two seconds. The swing is over by the time the first thought has come through the nervous system and registered with the part of the body it was addressed to. The golfer only has a dim recollection or feel for what actually happened, because he or she was thinking about what should have happened next.

When I ask students, 'What happened there. What did that feel like?' Often they answer: 'I'm not sure, I couldn't really feel it.'

The remedy is not to suggest something different, or to try harder, but to encourage the student to raise their awareness levels so they can feel what is happening. If they struggle to do this while swinging at full speed, they can slow down to a point where they can feel what is going on. The swing will speed up again once they raise their awareness levels.

A golfer starts to become independent when they can feel what is happening in the swing in real time. When that happens, students become their own coaches and are on the path to owning their own golf swing. External advice is less important once golfers achieve a superior awareness of their own swing.

Modern technology makes it so much easier for golfers to interpret the relationship between the movement of the body and the interaction between ball and clubface. High speed video cameras and sophisticated launch monitors such as GC2 and Trakman offer massive learning opportunities when data feedback is combined with that from our own senses.

I believe it's no coincidence that some of the great ball strikers of the past had little regular golf coaching. Lee Trevino, Sam Snead, Ben Hogan and Moe Norman were mainly self taught. Jack Nicklaus saw his mentor Jack Grout perhaps once a year. This is a far cry from many of today's tour players who have an entourage of coaches and advisors telling them what to think and do.

Learning must come from inside out if you want to own your own golf swing. Awareness is the key to this learning process. Curiosity about parts of your game you have the least feeling for is the gateway to awareness. This curiosity becomes a never ending quest, and is truly the path to mastery.

Trusting Your Swing.

You often hear a golfer after a great performance say, 'I just trusted my swing'. It sounds like a cliché to most handicap golfers. It's a concept they can't understand because they are so far away from trusting their own swing. It has let them down on numerous occasions. They have lost faith in it.

Most people feel frustrated after a poor golf shot because they don't really know why the poor shot happened. It's no surprise golfers feel they'll hit more bad shots when they have no idea why they hit bad shots in the first place. They're in the 'two shots from being crazy' scenario Fred Shoemaker describes in Extraordinary Golf. He goes on to write insightfully about the nature of trust in relation to the golf swing.

How do we learn to trust our own swing? What is the first step?

You only feel what's happening in your golf swing if you have high levels of awareness. Awareness creates a win-win situation. You'll understand why you hit a good shot. If you hit a poor shot, you will feel the difference, something that wasn't the same as that which produced the good one. You have learnt something!

You can get curious about the feeling, explore that feeling and where it comes from. Gradually the law of awareness will eliminate blind spots. This process builds trust. It is much easier to trust your swing if you can feel what is happening while it is happening.

I've always found reaction sports, where the ball is moving, easier to learn than golf. In tennis we react to the ball. We don't have time to think. Our instincts take over and we hit the ball. The shot may not be perfect, but we hit it. As we hit more shots, our natural learning abilities help us progress and improve. Crucially, we start to trust our instincts, our hand eye coordination, the innate learning process, and to trust ourselves.

We have more time to think when we're learning to play golf. We become less instinctive. When we hit a good shot, it seems like our thinking made it happen, so we try to think our way through the next shot. If we hit a bad shot we believe it must have been because we weren't thinking properly, so we change our thoughts. We never give our instincts a chance. We override the natural learning process, so trust in that process never develops.

Children are generally trusting before they learn to doubt. Is trust attributable to a clear mind, inner wisdom or a lack of intellect? Maybe, but it goes deeper. We automatically regain trust in our instincts when we learn to stop regarding every passing thought as important. If you act on a thought, despite a feeling of insecurity, because it contradicts your common sense, the result is unlikely to be good. Consequently, you become mistrustful of your own judgement, your instinctive abilities and your innate talent. This is a tragedy.

Insecure thinking is what we should learn to distrust. We don't make the connection between thoughts and mistrustful feelings because thoughts seem real. When we understand how thinking is created, we stop paying attention to every passing thought. We stop messing up, we stop feeling insecure, and we begin to trust ourselves again. We restore the connection with our inner wisdom.

Fixing the Yips.

Like many golfers, I've occasionally suffered from the yips. I remember putting from forty yards off the green while playing the first stage of European Tour Qualifying School at the Oxfordshire because I was scared of missing the ball with a wedge. It's generally been my short game, but occasionally with putting too. I tried various cures. I changed my putter, my grip, putted with my eyes closed and looked at the hole when I putted. These methods had varying success, but none provided a lasting solution.

I believe the yips come from an overload of thinking. Paralysis by analysis. It felt like my brain would shut down when I was about to hit the putt. My mind was saying: 'I can't deal with this much thought. Let's just get this over with.' So the shot took place in a mental blackout. I become unconscious for a split second while my body did its best to sort out the confused signals emanating from my brain. I had no recollection of what I did to hit the ball. I would then 'wake up' to see the result – which usually wasn't great, and the sorry saga repeated over the next putt.

Seemingly easy shots can be difficult for some people because there is less opportunity for creativity. Rather than being absorbed in creating something great, our thoughts are all about what could go wrong. Awareness levels can drop if we begin to fight against the flow of thinking.

Often people complain about 'losing concentration' when they miss a short putt. What do they mean? They are aware something went wrong, that they weren't fully present. Lack of awareness is the correct diagnosis. They were caught up in thought.

The problem comes on the next short putt. They tell themselves to concentrate or focus. You can't force yourself to concentrate or focus. When you try, you over think, you try to force something that can only happen naturally. You get bound up and tight, leading to another jerky, flinchy stroke.

Tim Gallwey states: *'Awareness is curative.'* I make no apology for repeating this quote. Just by being aware of something in your swing, the body will naturally make the necessary adjustments to ensure that the movement is successful, that it improves and becomes more efficient. Awareness is at the core of the natural, Inside Out way we learn movement, and perform that movement with ease and grace.

Awareness was the remedy for my inconsistency on the putting green. I spent some time just rolling the ball to nothing, no target, no hole. I had some thinking going on about holing putts. I actually had very little idea what the putter was doing during my stroke, or what part of my body was tightening up causing the flinch.

As I rolled ball after ball, my stroke gradually got longer and smoother without trying to make any conscious technical changes. I simply got curious about how the putter was moving back and through the ball. I felt my hands relax and I started to feel the weight of the putter head swinging again.

My putting has been much better since I made curiosity my main focus on the putting green. It's a much nicer feeling than trying hard and worrying about whether I'm going to hole putts. I'm enjoying the process of putting rather than feeling anxious and insecure. Inevitably, my form sometimes dips. There are times when I feel the ball isn't coming off the blade solidly. Sometimes my feel for distance is poor. My awareness levels have dropped and performance suffers. Then I realise I've started thinking about results. Once I get curious about process again, I'm back on track.

Consciousness is Infinite.

> 'You will never come to the end of Consciousness, because Consciousness is infinite – there is no end to it. That is a beautiful thing to know, because it means to say there is no end to you finding beauty, love and understanding in this world.'
>
> —Syd Banks

I love this quote. Seeing the infinite nature of Consciousness is the key to remaining fascinated with golf for the rest of your life. You can always go deeper than you currently are. Golf is often a lifelong love affair because it has many different facets to learn and improve: driving, iron shots, pitching, chipping, bunker shots, putting, course management and the inner game.

You need a range of skills and attributes to play golf well: touch, control, power, speed, balance, patience, calmness and resilience. Awareness is the best route to learning to playing consistently well. Awareness is also the key to remaining fascinated with the game because it is infinite.

Consciousness, is vertical rather than horizontal. The doorway is curiosity. Once you step inside you can always find higher of levels of consciousness. You can always become more aware. Fred Shoemaker suggests respective levels of awareness are the main difference between tour players and average golfers.

Tour players understandably practice more than most amateurs. They will stay on the practice ground long after regular golfers have got bored and gone home. How do they stay interested? How do they avoid getting burnt out and stale?

By staying curious, by going deeper into awareness of what they are doing.

Most amateurs assume tour players grind away because they have to. I've spent a few thousand hours on practice ranges in my time. In my experience, great golfers are hitting balls because they love doing it. They are absorbed and fascinated by the interaction between themselves, the club and the ball.

They just love playing golf and are curious to see if they can play even better. We will explore where the feeling of love for the game originates in the next chapter. In the meantime, I promise that your enjoyment will increase as awareness of what you're doing when you play and practice increases.

Consciousness, awareness of what we are doing, determines the quality of our experience. My experience of my golf swing is deeper, richer, more detailed and more enjoyable when my levels of awareness are high compared to when my consciousness is low and I'm just going through the motions.

Some days I am so aware that I can feel every single inch of my golf swing, almost as if it is happening in slow motion. I feel the club change direction at the top, my weight shift, the club drop into the slot and accelerate through to collect the ball right out of the centre of the club. I feel the solidness of the impact, and look up to see the ball flying straight at the flagstick. This state is the most satisfying feeling in the whole game, and my most important reason for playing.

This, to me, is the Zone.

Finding 'The Zone.'

Awareness, or Consciousness, is the principle which allows us to feel our body moving the club during the golf swing. We feel the weight of the clubhead, the resistance from the ground as we turn and pivot and the way our body moves during the swing. Awareness allows us to feel the ball being struck, and to hear and see it soaring up and away towards the target.

Awareness allows us to appreciate the beauty of the golf courses we play on, and enjoy the scenery those golf courses are part of. Happily, awareness is a natural, familiar, easy state for us to find as we swing, once we know where to look for it.

Human beings are naturally curious. When we become curious, our awareness of a subject, or object or movement naturally increases. Curiosity leads to awareness, awareness leads to fascination, fascination leads to absorption. When we become absorbed in what we are doing, it is one of the most productive and pleasurable states a human being can attain.

It is a state of no thought, of pure Consciousness, of bliss. When sports people talk about this state, they sometimes call it The Zone. Our performance levels are higher the more time we spend in this state, and the more we enjoy what we are doing.

When golfers talk about concentration or focus, what they are really experiencing is an elevated Awareness. If you become deeply aware, you are concentrating. When you hold your attention on something, your awareness has risen. You are focused on it.

You Can't 'Do Awareness.'

I need to add a warning at this point. I fell into a trap when I first learned about awareness after reading 'The Inner Game' in the early 1990s. I imagine a few other golfers have fallen for it too.

Awareness comes naturally when you get curious about something. It isn't a practice or a technique you can force or achieve with willpower. You'll know exactly what I am talking about if you have ever found yourself trying to concentrate or focus over a golf shot. You can no more will yourself to concentrate or focus on the shot than you can will yourself to fall asleep. The more you try, the more your thinking revs up, and the further you stray from the calm, clear state of awareness you seek.

Awareness is natural. It happens when you start no- ticing something in your golf swing, when you get curious about it. Thought slows down as awareness increases. The opposite happens when you start from a mind set of trying to be aware. Any form of conscious mental manipulation (thinking) about something we do naturally will usually produce poor results. This is why deliberate mindfulness or meditation doesn't work for everyone.

Relaxation, concentration, awareness, clarity all happen naturally. Consciousness will rise with no work or effort when you get curious. Your thinking will slow down and will recede into the background.

Let Your Feelings Guide You.

Your feelings are your guide to whether you are looking in the right direction – inside, towards your instincts and common sense, or outside, for intellectual answers or techniques. Your consciousness will stay high when you feel free, relaxed and absorbed in what you're doing. By contrast, you may feel tight or anxious if you're working at awareness, willing yourself to focus or concentrate. You'll feel you're off track.

When I read 'Golf is Not a Game of Perfect', I followed Bob Rotella's advice to 'focus on a small target.' It wasn't till I learned to be more aware of what I was feeling, that I realised how tense trying to 'focus on a small target' made me feel. I felt my perceptual field closing and my tension levels rising when I started to focus on the flag or a tree branch in the distance, or a spot on the green or inside the cup.

It felt more natural and I swung more freely when I looked at the whole of the green and noticed what a huge area I had to hit the ball into. I let my eyes find the flag, got curious about where I felt the target was when I looked back to the ball and let the shot find the target.

I'm not saying my method is right, or that picking a

small target is wrong. If picking a small target works for you, if you feel calm, swing freely and and the ball goes where you want, keep doing it. I'm saying my feelings were telling me about my state of mind in the moment.

This is why prescribing techniques or following someone else's strategy can be dangerous. Anxious or insecure feelings should be warning signals that your thinking isn't working for you. How you feel is always your truest guide. The important lesson is knowing what your feelings are telling you.

Passing judgment on what you're doing or on your results is another sign that you are slipping from awareness into thinking. Perhaps you have a blind spot in a certain part of your swing. You get curious about that particular area or a part of your body and feel it isn't moving smoothly. Rather than just observing and allowing the learning process to happen, we make the next swing and fall into the trap of judging whether the move we made was good or bad, right or wrong.

Awareness, like thought, is completely neutral. What's happening at any given moment can always be interesting and instructive, rather than good or bad. You will probably experience an uneasy feeling when you label something as bad or negative. You are slipping out of awareness into judging. Thought has been added to the process. When this happens just get curious again, maybe in the same area of your swing, maybe in something different, and let yourself get absorbed back into the experience of what you were doing.

Awareness, consciousness in action, is a fine cure for

the majority of golfing ills. Raising your awareness levels will quieten your mind. It will help you stay relaxed and in the moment when you play.

Raising your awareness levels when practising or taking a lesson will help you find the blind spots in your swing or putting stroke. Getting curious about those blind spots will allow the curative power of awareness to go to work, subtly changing and refining those areas without struggling, grinding or working.

Realising that consciousness is infinite allows you to go ever deeper into your golf game, uncovering and understanding its hidden details and secrets.

Increased awareness is the road to mastery, to owning your golf swing. It's the reason the great ball strikers are rarely bored, rarely feel over golfed. They stay fascinated by the game, always curious to find out how deep they can go and how good they can be.

The awesome feeling of total absorption in the process, is the reason Arnold Palmer and Ben Hogan hit balls almost every day long after they finished playing for a living.

You, too, can remain fascinated by the game for the rest of your days if you begin to look in the direction of awareness and curiosity, and you will play some outstanding golf in the meantime.

CHAPTER 7

Gain Control by Giving Up Control.

'We are not human beings having a spiritual experience. We are spiritual beings having a human experience'.

—*Pierre Teillhard de Chardin*

THIS CHAPTER WAS CHALLENGING TO WRITE. It's pointing to a phenomenon that cannot be described. It can only be felt. When you feel something and are moved by it, the temptation is to put it into an intellectual context, to describe it. The principle of Mind is something that can only really be understood with your heart and soul. Try to explain the feeling of a purely struck golf shot to someone who has never played golf before, it's hard to find words to do it justice. Unlike a golf shot, every human being has felt what I'm pointing towards at some point in their lives. This chapter will help you find it and stay in it more often.

There are ideas, questions and concepts in the following paragraphs which some people may find uncomfortable. It may be difficult to see their relevance to golf. I was advised to edit this chapter, or leave it out altogether. This advice was welcome, it forced me to make sure an important message is conveyed in a form that will hopefully be accessible to as many people as possible.

There are numerous reasons why this chapter remains. From a personal perspective, the acceptance of the possibility that I couldn't control what happened on the golf course was another big step towards feeling calm, in control of my emotions, and at peace with myself, instead of nervous, doubtful and insecure.

I was familiar with the phrase 'to gain control you have to give up control', but didn't really understand what it meant. One of the reasons I loved golf was precisely because, as an individual sport, I thought I was in control of my own effort. Winning or losing was down to me and me alone, or so I believed. This was liberating in one sense, but compounded my feelings of pressure and anxiety in another.

Understanding the principle of Mind gave me a completely different perception of what it means to be in control, and why seeing the balance between responsibility and freedom is so important for a golfer. It metaphorically blew my mind wide open, stripping away layers of thinking that had been impairing my capacity to play my best golf and to enjoy it. This huge insight simplified the way I saw the game of golf and changed the way I feel on the golf course for ever.

There is another important reason why this chapter is important. Without understanding the principle of Mind, the other two principles, Thought and Consciousness, become just another mental strategy to apply which may or may not give temporary relief from insecure feelings, lack of trust and a lack of confidence many golfers are familiar with.

The Three Principles are like a three-legged stool. Take one of the legs away and what's left isn't much use. By understanding all three elements, you can find feelings of hope and optimism whenever you look inside yourself rather than outside for answers. Mental strength and mental resilience are elevated to previously un-known levels when a golfer feels the true nature of Mind.

To feel the benefit of these words, please put aside everything you think you're searching for and everything you think you know. Try to keep an open mind. Don't try to compare these ideas with other concepts or philosophies you might be familiar with. You picked up this book because you want to become a better golfer. You already are a better golfer. You will see why later in the chapter.

If you can put your desire for improvement on the back burner for a few minutes, your feeling for what I'm pointing to will become much deeper. It will help you in more ways than you can think of intellectually. You won't understand what I'm saying with your intellectual mind. When you do start to become aware of it, you'll feel it.

If you can sense the feeling behind what the words are saying and keep your mind clear and free, something wonderful may happen. You'll feel a calmness, relaxa-tion, stillness, and a sense of peace. Your thinking will slow down and your intellect will go quiet. You will go beyond Thought. You will feel your connection to Mind, to your inner wisdom beginning to open up. Insights will begin to flow, and your life and golf will start to feel very different.

The Big Question.

In the preceding chapters, we looked into the nature of Consciousness, how we create and experience reality, what we mean by the present moment and whether the flow of time actually happens. Now we are going to look at what might be behind the origins of the universe itself. I understand this is a weighty topic for a book supposedly about getting better at hitting a ball with a stick.

I'm addressing this fundamental question because I believe many golfers want to understand more about why they play and what golf means to them. To do that, we need to look more deeply at ourselves, our deeper nature and what moves us, rather than just at the game of golf.

I love golf because on the surface it is very simple. The longer I play, the more intriguing and complex the game becomes, and the more it captivates me. Some golfers are happy just to play, have fun and not think too deeply about why they play. If you fit into this category, that's fine. I'm a bit envious in a way. However, I guess if you're that sort of golfer, you wouldn't have got this far into the book.

Once you start to ask questions about why you play, and the true relevance of the game to your life and your fellow golfers, you can find out some pretty profound and important things about yourself and about other people. This is how I got to where I am now.

This road of discovery can be a rocky one, and is not a journey all golfers want to take. For those that do, it can be a significant step towards reaching your true potential. You probably spend a considerable amount of valuable leisure time and your hard earned cash pursuing your hobby. I may be contradicting my own advice to avoid analysis and introspection, but surely it's worth a few minutes of contemplation to understand why the game of golf grips us in the way it does?

Universal Intelligence.

It appears that our world is formed from matter. It seems solid. We can see it, touch it, feel it. But as we have discovered, reality isn't always as it seems. Quantum physics tells us that matter is formed from energy. The more we explore the building blocks of the universe, we find that even the most solid of objects is in fact formed from swarming particles and waves of energy.

Syd Banks describes Mind as a spiritual energy, the intelligence behind the creation of the universe and everything in it. This energy is the source we all came from, and what we will all go back to after we hit our final shot. If you are looking for a line marking the frontier between the physical and the spiritual, it is becoming easier to argue that it is lightly sketched, rather than heavily inked.

Physics tells us that energy isn't created or destroyed, it just changes form. The transfer of energy from one form to another is an interesting concept for golfers to consider. It happens every time we hit a shot.

The energy that makes a golf ball fly through the air is imparted by the movement of your golf club. The energy swinging the golf club comes from the movement of your body. Your body generates the energy to move from the food you eat. The food was grown using the energy of the sun.

The trail starts to get less well marked at this point. The sun is a sphere of burning gas, mainly hydrogen. Where did the gas that burns in the sun, come from? What were the forces that formed the sun and the other billions of stars in the universe? Where did that energy come from?

There are a number of theories, including the 'Big Bang,' an explosion thought to be the origin of every-thing in the universe as we know it, but as yet, there is no definitive explanation. A recent quantum equation based on the work of David Bohm, suggests that there is no beginning to the universe. It has existed forever. It is infinite, both in scope and duration.

Charles Darwin, whose theory of evolution stands as the most widely accepted scientific explanation of how human beings came to be as we are today, wrote:

'The mystery of the beginning of all things is insoluble by us; and I for one must be content to remain an ag-nostic.'

What we can say with certainty, is that the small amount of energy you used to roll in that four-footer to win the medal last week didn't originate with you. You didn't create it. It manifested through you. Its origins were perhaps millions of light years away, billions of years ago, if indeed it had origins at all.

You might want to ponder on that for a moment.

Considering the chaos and confusion surrounding the origins of the universe, and the journey this planet has been on since, it could easily be seen as a miracle that the environment we inhabit is so benign, well ordered and accommodating. Consider the nature of the elements, plants and organisms which combine in perfect harmony to allow your favourite golf course to exist. You might wonder how they came to be there, and why they are the way they are, the perfect setting for you to play your favourite game?

For centuries, wise men have marvelled at the 'kindness of the design' we see around us in nature. It isn't surprising that for centuries men have wondered about whether there might be an 'intelligence behind life'.

Philosopher Aristotle wrote;

'In all things of nature, there is something of the marvellous.

The father of modern physics, Albert Einstein wrote of a 'cosmic religious feeling', which was fundamental to the progress of both art and science. He said of 'the scientist' (one assumes he was including himself in that category),

'His religious feeling takes the form of rapturous amazement at the harmony of natural law, which re-

veals an intelligence of such superiority that, compared with it, all the systematic thinking and acting of human beings is an utterly insignificant reflection.'

I can understand the scepticism around the existence of a spiritual intelligence or universal energy. I have no proof. But many people I share this idea with have a sense of it, a feeling about it. They have an awareness that there is something both 'out there' and 'inside' them, a powerful capability that they sometimes feel directly connected to. This feeling is proof enough if our goal is simply to live a life we love.

There are many examples of sportsmen and women describing the feeling that an exceptional performance did not originate with them. They had the sense it flowed through them, just as the energy we use to hit a golf ball is part of the flow of energy around the universe.

When I write about spiritual intelligence, some people jump to the conclusion that I mean God in a religious sense. They have their own ideas and concepts of what God means and represents. These thoughts can engender strong feelings. Britain is home to an increasingly secular society, and indifference, even hostility towards organised religion is commonplace. The reasons are varied, but it seems fewer people find relevance in the messages the main religions offer. No one likes being judged and told what to think and how to live their lives.

On the other side, those with strong religious beliefs have become more strident and evangelical, and in extreme cases seek to impose their version of what they believe to be the truth on others.

This polarisation of attitudes towards religion is frustrating. Discussion about some of the richest, most profound, most fundamental feelings human beings experience – unconditional love, spiritual intelligence, elevated states of consciousness, the connection to our fellow men and women, to nature and to the planet we inhabit, often descends into argument about the pro's and cons of a primitive, three-thousand-year old theology.

This reluctance to look inside ourselves has created mental no go areas, discouraging people from wondering where these feelings originate. Insecure thinking about organised religion contaminates the discussion about the nature of the human experience and what these deep and inspiring feelings might mean for us as individuals, and as a society.

When I gave friends an early draft of this book, this chapter got a mixed response. Some didn't understand it, others were curious. Some said they found it helpful. Several told me they didn't want to read about spiritual ideas in a golf book. A few with strong religious beliefs regard the ideas I'm putting forward as blasphemous, because they question the fundamental teachings of their particular faith.

None of these comments are wrong, but they're not right either. They're thoughts, personal opinions. Whether someone agrees or disagrees doesn't depend on the truth of what Syd Banks is pointing to, his description of the nature of human experience. It depends on what their personal beliefs, their thoughts about it are.

If you are starting to feel agitated, frustrated or con-fused by these ideas, it might help if you go back and reread Chapter Five. Reassess on where those feelings are coming from. If you're still feeling calm and your mind is open, I'll sum up what we learned there in the context of this chapter.

Like any other belief, religious beliefs are thoughts. Personal thoughts. For some people, these thoughts engender feelings of comfort, peace of mind and faith.

For other people, thoughts about religion provoke very much the opposite feelings: scepticism, cynicism, hostility and doubt.

The feelings whether positive or negative, come from their thinking, not from books, or churches or events or from other people who believe something different from them.

Religion and 'God' are not the same thing. Religion is a signpost. It isn't what the signpost is pointing to. If you want to call Spiritual Intelligence 'God', and it fits in with your current religious beliefs, that's beautiful. If the word 'God' has connotations you don't like, or feel uncomfort-able with, and you prefer Human Spirit, Nature, Soul, Wisdom or Life Source, please use the words which make sense to you.

I use the word 'Mind' because that is the word Syd Banks used. However, he also said after his experience of enlightenment, (much to the surprise and in some cases disapproval of his close friends,) that he had seen 'God'. The words we use to point to this spiritual intelligence are irrelevant. What is important is the feeling of peace and oneness that comes with knowing that we are connected to something greater than ourselves. We belong to it, we came from it and we will go back to it.

'All the major religions of the world, they all have the answer, but it's hidden. It's hidden in a maze of thoughts, ideas and concepts. There's no idea or concept in the world which holds the truth.'

—Syd Banks

Where Does Golf Fit In All This?

Why is understanding the principle of Mind so important when we feel frustrated by the game, when we are feeling anxious and insecure? How will it help us play better? How can a 'spiritual intelligence' help us when we are on the golf course and are feeling like the game is getting the better of us?

Previously when I felt things were going against me, I would've tried to dig in, grind it out, use my willpower or reach for a coping technique or mental strategy. I might have played a bit better for a while, but I certainly wouldn't have felt better. If anything I'd have felt worse.

It's easy to take golf personally. The nature of the game means we feel solely responsible for our results and our performance. We have no teammates to cover for us or share responsibility when things go wrong. We have no opponent who can physically prevent us performing to our potential or impose his game on ours so we can't blame anyone for not playing to the best of our ability. It is a contest with the golf course and ourselves. When things don't work out, it looks like it's down to us. It's easy to feel that the game is against us.

It's hard to remember that how we feel about golf depends on our thoughts. It's easy for our thinking to rev up when things go badly and there is no one to help us. We blame ourselves for our bad results, our bad play. We take it personally. I know I did for a long time. I spent hours beating myself up when I hit a bad shot or played a bad round. It's easy to see why many people feel that golf is the toughest of all sports from a mental perspective.

Realising the principle of Mind allowed me to make sense of the concept that 'we gain control by giving up control.' My first insight was a simple acceptance that the game isn't meant to be fair. We get bad bounces, sometimes good shots end up in bad places. We often forget that it works the other way round too.

I began to feel that I could back off a bit. I gave myself the benefit of the doubt sometimes, stopped thinking I could, or needed to control everything. I began to feel less stressed. I stopped taking it personally. I started being kinder to myself. I gave myself a break. It was as simple as admitting, 'It's not totally down to me anymore; what will be will be.' I relaxed a bit more. My game started to come back. I started to enjoy it again.

How I got to this place was critical. It wasn't a license to start making excuses or blaming other people or circumstances for how I felt. We shouldn't stop trying because it doesn't look like being our day.

I mentioned in Chapter Five that 'giving up' as a strategy for coping with feelings of pressure doesn't work. It decreases the motivation for playing, and goes against our natural instincts to give our best and play as well as we can. I felt negative, careless and demotivated when I first tried to 'give up control'. What was I giving it up to? If I'm not in control, what or who is? Is something else now in control of me? That idea went against one of the tenets I held most strongly, my free will.

Giving Up Control – to Ourselves.

The answer to the question 'who is in control?' is found in the formless essence of the Three Principles. The answer is inside all of us. We all have a place in our minds which is literally 'beyond belief'. You can think of this space as pure consciousness, before the contamination of thought, of our beliefs, ideas of what or who we are, what we can or can't do.

It's the place where our inner wisdom merges with the spiritual intelligence behind all of life. It's the place where miracles come from. There are no words to describe it, no intellectual concept that can come close to doing it justice. Certainly no religion can lay claim to it. The only way we can know it, is by trusting that it is there and feeling its effects.

When we decide to give up intellectual control, we tap into this space. We put our faith and trust in a power greater than what we conceive of as our own, even though it is within us. We stop limiting ourselves in terms of what we think we are capable of.

When a golfer produces a performance beyond what they thought was possible, they are playing from this place. Universal intelligence manifests as their inner wisdom. They find themselves in the zone, and they play to a level they could only dream about.

You may hear golfers who have strong religious beliefs espouse that their exceptional play was bestowed upon them by God. They may thank a higher power. They aren't wrong, and if that feeling works for them, by all means keep believing. The performance wasn't gifted to them by a benevolent divine entity. It came from a place inside them. It came through them, not from anything outside. You will wait a long time for an omnipotent deity to hit a golf shot for you.

A golfer may feel they found the zone because they gave up intellectual control of what they were doing. In that sense, again they're correct. It wasn't their intellect or conscious mind that produced the performance. It came from the psychological space before thought, beyond belief. It came from Mind. For me, being connected to Mind is the simple feeling of walking onto a golf course with no thought or belief I need to 'think something,' 'do something' or 'feel something' in order to play well and enjoy the experience.

The wisest, sanest, calmest, most humble people I know, have a deep sense that they aren't in control of what happens. They have a clear vision of their role in how life plays out. They understand there is a spiritual dimension to the universe, the planet, and to every other living thing. Many are not religious in the sense they don't go to church. They don't read religious books. They draw their strength from inside themselves rather than from something outside.

They are at their happiest when they are helping others, rather than focused on their own achievements. It may look from outside as if they are living in accordance with a religion or philosophy, but only because religion points us to the same place, the place we already know. They are simply living from their own inner wisdom.

As I said earlier, you will either get a feeling for what I'm pointing to, or you won't. It will mean something to you or will seem confusing, irrelevant. If you take one thing from this chapter, please let it be the certain knowledge that our natural state of being is to feel content, happy, loving and at peace. We are allowed to enjoy and love what we do. We feel at ease when our personal thinking subsides.

The 'no pain, no gain' philosophy, the idea that we must suffer in order to one day be to be free, to be 'something', has no basis in fact. Long ago, someone made that story up. Millions have bought into it and are suffering because of it.

Peace of mind is our natural state. It's where we live. If you dwell mainly in this state of mind just keep doing what you are doing. Whether you realise it or not, you are connected to the spiritual intelligence, to wisdom. You are living from that space within you which is the real you, before thought, before belief. You're living from your soul.

On the other hand, if you feel some stress, pressure, anxiety, insecurity about your golf or anything else. If you feel lost, that you're searching for something, if you feel that something is missing, please look in the one place you probably haven't looked yet. Look deeper inside.

"The most beautiful experience we can have is the mysterious. It is the fundamental emotion that stands at the cradle of true art and true science."

—Albert Einstein.

What Golf Means to Me.

What really matters to most golfers is how we feel when we play. I'm trying to describe a feeling, an expression of our existence that cannot be put into words. This feeling is formless. As soon as I put it into words it is no longer what it is. In summing up the principle of Mind, I'm pointing towards something beyond a simple game we play with a ball and a stick.

The game might seem trivial, especially to people who have never played. But golf is a vital part of life for many of us. It is our recreation, our main form of play, our connection with the great outdoors, with nature, our path back to the source of life itself. It's an important part of the social fabric of our lives, a way of enjoying the company of like-minded people. It's completely meaningless and absolutely fundamental at the same time.

It can feel like golf is a never-ending search. We're constantly trying to understand the game, find answers to why we play well, why we play badly, why certain shots go where we intended and others don't. The problem is, when we find answers to these questions, there are always new ones. We feel insecure and lost if we are always searching.

The way I enjoy the game and feel at ease with myself is to become comfortable with not knowing. After all, we would lose interest fairly quickly if we knew exactly how each round was going to unfold. A big part of the attraction of golf is the unknown. The intellect doesn't really like not knowing. We like to have it all figured out. Wisdom on the other hand is fine with the unknown. Wisdom is the unknown.

All the way through the book, but especially in this chapter, I have gone off the beaten path a few times. The main point I'm trying to get across is that none of the answers we seek are 'out there'. They aren't in science and technology. They aren't in religion or philosophy, or in someone else's intellectual knowledge. They aren't in biomechanics, golf lessons, training aids, books or instruction videos.

Your answers are right here. Inside you.

This is why understanding the principle of Mind was so helpful to me. It points us Inside, to what matters most about being human, towards some of the most fundamentally satisfying feelings we can experience. It offers us a chance to understand and simplify our reasons for playing golf. It explains our up and down feelings about the game, and why it draws us back despite the frustrations, false dawns and dashed hopes.

It's why after 30 years of being around the game, I'm still as fascinated today as when I first started chipping a ball around my parents' garden. The feeling of knowing I am connected to Mind is such a beautiful experience, I'm sure I will keep being fascinated for the next thirty years.

CHAPTER 8

Golf Is A Mind And Body Game.

'We cannot solve our problems with the same thinking we used when we created them.'

—*Albert Einstein*

THIS BOOK IS PRIMARILY ABOUT the mental side of the game. However, golf is a mind and body game. I'll never say that technique isn't important. I spend a lot of my time helping golfers improve their swings and spent years improving my own. Simply put, good technique is more efficient than bad technique. However, there is a balance to be struck between functional and optimal.

The time you have available and your physical conditioning will be factors in how far you go in your search for perfection. It is important to make an honest assessment of whether you need to change your technique. As well as pursuing a long term objective of improving their golf swing, most golfers want to enjoy their game and play the best golf they are capable of doing now.

There is a simple test to decide whether improving your technique should be a priority. If you can hit the shots you want to hit when you are feeling calm and relaxed, then your technique is functional. If you don't hit the same quality of shots when you are feeling nervous or 'under pressure', you will get more leverage in terms of improvement by addressing your state of mind, not your swing.

One of the biggest mistakes I see golfers make, is believing they should get their swing technique sorted before they fully understand how their mind really works. From my own personal experience this is very much the hard way of doing it. I spent years grinding and trying to build a golf swing which would stand up under pressure. Unfortunately it's people who succumb to pressure, not golf swings. Once you understand the relationship between thought and feeling, you will play your best golf more often, and you will learn faster and with less effort as well.

Learn the Easy Way.

No matter how good you become at golf, there is always opportunity to improve your technique and capabilities. There are so many different elements, disciplines and skills to practice and improve. Every golfer will have an answer to the question, 'What are you working on?' Refining your golf swing to hit the ball further and straighter, or learning a new way of playing a shot is extremely satisfying. Hopefully the rest of this chapter will make it easier and less frustrating than you have found up to this point.

Improvement is inevitable when you play the game from the clear state of mind you are now learning about.

The Law of Awareness will take care of that. Your skills and technique will improve the moment your levels of consciousness begin to rise. You will discover blind spots in your swing and the areas that need improvement will become obvious. You will swing the club faster and with more consistency as you learn to trust yourself and let the movement flow. More of your innate ability will be revealed.

Be honest about why you want to make the change. Is it an authentic desire to find out how good you can be, or the notion that a good looking backswing will get a few compliments down the driving range? It's very easy to slip into the 'I'll Be Happy When Game' when you start thinking you need to make changes.

Learning is a natural, innate capability. Learning comes easily when you are calm and seeing things clearly. Finding a teacher who understands the inside out way we learn movement, and who has a good understanding of the golf swing will be an advantage.

Learn Your Golf Swing, Not Someone Else's.

The information overload described in Chapter Three manifests as too much thinking when the golfer goes to the practice ground or to the lesson tee. You might have read a golf magazine, or seen a video about the latest, 'best' way to swing a golf club, and now have thoughts about how to use this swing method. All this thinking gets in the way of feeling your golf swing, of becoming aware how *you* best swing the golf club.

I often make this statement in golf lessons: 'Your job

isn't to learn *the* golf swing, it's to learn *your* golf swing.' Information is different from understanding. We have masses of information available at the tap of a screen. We often think the answer to all our frustrations lies in learning something new, or accepting somebody else's thoughts about the swing. Understanding movement comes from feeling and doing. It comes from inside, not from applying somebody else's idea about what works for them. Learning something new is often an excuse for not doing what we already know we should be doing.

Learn to Move by Moving, Not by Thinking.

Learning to move is a natural and normal process for everyone. We are learning from the moment we are born. Walking, talking, running, brushing our teeth, driving a car, these are all examples of complex movement patterns we learn over a lifetime. We perform these tasks flawlessly with little conscious thought, day in day out.

Young children and young animals are voracious learners. Watch a child playing with a new toy for the first time, or two puppies play-fighting, and you have great role models for the learning experience. They aren't working at it, or trying to learn. They're having an exciting, interesting and stimulating experience. Learning is happening as a consequence of the game, without conscious thought or effort.

Trusting the natural learning process is the key. If I understand that excessive thinking can hinder my progress rather than help, I allow my curiosity to run free. I can explore possibilities of swinging any way I want without fear. I know at any point I can rein in my imagination and allow my mind to settle and clear, and my golf swing will return to its natural form.

If I don't know that thought is transient, if all my thinking looks real and important, I can get myself in a mess. I become attached to this thought or that thought, or believe I've found 'the secret', only to find it doesn't feel the same the next time I play. I find myself in a never ending loop of searching for the right intellectual answer. Alternatively I can look beyond my intellect, get quiet for a few minutes, allow my awareness levels to rise and get back to the way children learn – by playing, having fun and allowing the learning to happen in the background.

For Golf Instructors.

I love teaching, and I have great respect for my friends and colleagues who do the same. We are lucky to have a most rewarding, enjoyable way of earning a living. We get the chance to make a real difference to someone's life every day. Leisure time is precious in a busy world, too precious not to enjoy. We help people enjoy that time more by helping them become more proficient at the game they love.

If you've got this far in the book, I'm hoping you have a sense of what I'm saying about the way golf is taught. I'm not pointing fingers or criticising individual golf instructors. However, the way many golfers learn to play golf is too much like hard work and is ultimately ineffective. It has to change. Helping golfers learn how to learn, is arguably more important than what they learn.

Throughout the game's history, there have been any number of different ways to swing a golf club successfully. One size or one golf swing does not fit all. By pointing the golfer inwards towards their instincts, towards awareness, you can help them access a natural capacity for learning which has made human beings the most successful animal on the planet. Help them learn a golf swing which suits them, which works for them, rather than what what works for you or someone else.

When you tell golfers what to do, what to feel, what to think, when you point them towards theory and positions and routines, you are short-circuiting the natural learning system. You are helping them get in their own way. I know it's tempting to take short cuts, to give answers rather than asking questions. Heaven knows I've done it, but I've usually regretted it. It's hard to stop once you start down the outside in path. Instead of setting the golfer free, you create a dependency, unhealthy for both of you.

I understand the hard work involved in making a living as a golf teacher, of retaining clients and attracting new ones. I've experienced the ups and downs of that life. I'm very positive about the future. There are thousands of unhappy, frustrated golfers crying out for a better way of learning, a better way of playing, desperate to enjoy the game more. Your lesson diary will be overflowing if you concentrate on helping golfers become their own coaches. Set the individual client free as quickly as possible.

"The words that come out of a coach's mouth are far less important than the coach's state of mind when he says the words."

—*Garret Kramer*

For the golfer practicing or taking a lesson, it will help greatly if your mind is quiet and clear. The essence of effective learning is the same as the essence of effective performance on the golf course, or anywhere else. If you've ever had a golf lesson or a series of lessons that didn't work out the way you hoped, chances are your thinking was getting in the way.

It's easy to blame a lack of ability on your part, or a failure by the teacher to diagnose the problem or communicate a solution. The quality of our thinking determines our state of mind, not our situation or circumstances as is routinely assumed. Equally important, and often overlooked by both student and teacher, is the coach's state of mind during a lesson. If the coach isn't aware of his low level of consciousness, an unproductive lesson and frustration on both sides is the likely outcome.

When a student comes into the studio I can often tell straight away if he or she has a busy mind and a lot of thinking going on. It's often the first thing I notice and I make allowances. Taking a lesson can be quite a stressful experience for many people.

When you know about the link between thought, feeling and behaviour, you just get a sense when someone has a lot on their mind. The worst thing I can do is start giving the student even more to think about. I might have the best insight in the world, something that will really help them, but at that moment my observation will just get lost in the clutter.

Once they have hit balls for a few minutes and their thinking starts to quieten down, I might ask a question about how their swing is feeling. At this point they will be able to feel any changes in their swing and improvement will happen much more easily.

Awareness of my own level of consciousness during a lesson is important. Whether I'm seeing things clearly, and whether I'm really hearing what the golfer is saying depends on my state of mind. In some of the best lessons I've given I've said very little. I've just pointed the golfer towards awareness, suggested he or she gets curious and let their inner wisdom take over. Change follows. I've asked a couple of questions about a new feeling in the swing. The student is able to explain the difference and improvement takes place. More importantly, the student finds the process very comfortable. That's it.

The feeling is spiritual, almost magical when these moments occur. Two people in a high state of consciousness and connection working towards a shared purpose. Most teachers will have experienced this phenomenon at some point.

Most of us have experienced this absorption, this total immersion in a task and in the moment. This is learning in its purest, most effective form. It isn't hard work. We aren't grinding, or trying hard. It feels effortless, free and completely natural. This is how a golf lesson, a practice session or a round of golf should feel.

Why Is It So Hard to Change A Golf Swing?

I believe the answer lies in the nature of thought. In Chapter Five I described how thought is the missing link between our circumstances and how we feel. Much of the time, we aren't aware of our thinking.

Setting aside certain primitive and essential biological functions such as breathing and the heart pumping blood around the body, all human activity begins with a thought. There is a psychological impulse or intention which causes the muscles to move. So if a movement has occurred, there must have been a thought which caused it to happen.

> 'Muscles do not move on their own; they need to be stimulated in order to move. They have no brain, no mind, so they cannot have any memory. They simply do what they are told through our mental processes. To produce a specific movement they must not only be stimulated for movement, but this stimulation must be directed so the muscles produce the movement desired. Without this direction, the movements produced will vary greatly, and most likely be incorrect for the desired result.'
>
> —Manuel de la Torre. Understanding The Golf Swing

Intention is an important concept for the golfer to understand. The only reason anyone does anything, is because at that particular moment in time, it seemed like a good idea. It made sense to them in that moment. Similarly, the reason we don't do something, even if we know that we should do it, is because we have a subsequent thought which suggests it isn't such a good idea, and we shouldn't act on that thought after all. We have all experienced this pattern of thinking when we procrastinate and make excuses.

Most important of all to understand, is that our thinking, our intentions can look very different depending on our level of consciousness.

Our intentions standing over a golf shot can be revealing. It's not unusual to have different, sometimes conflicting thoughts standing over the same shot. It seems to me that our thinking occurs at different levels of consciousness. We have quite obvious, ephemeral levels of thought, part of the minute to minute flow of cognition and ideas. We are aware of these thoughts, and we often react to them, particularly if we aren't aware that we are the one thinking them. We might call this intellectual thought.

We also have deep, well established beliefs and patterns of thinking, which are almost subconscious, at levels we are not so aware of from moment to moment. We may not always be aware enough to recognise these thoughts, but they must still happen in the background.

It seems to me that these deeper levels of thinking are more powerful in the way they translate into behaviour, particularly when looking at movement. Take a golfer who hits a high, weak slice. That golfer might well know at an intellectual level, that he should get his hands on the golf club in a correct neutral grip. Somehow, in the moment of setting up to the shot, the club ends up in the palm of the left hand and the right hand gets turned too far to the right.

This golfer also knows he shouldn't spin his shoulders and throw the club out and away from him from the top of the backswing, but he can't seem to stop himself from acting on the impulse to do it.

Your intellectual thoughts may be clear in terms of what you want to do with a golf shot. You can visualise a high draw as much as you like. Your intellectual thoughts and good intentions won't help if you have an ingrained pattern of thinking which, at a subconscious level, tells your body to throw the club out and down towards the ball at the start of the downswing.

Fortunately, this dynamic works in our favour when the movement is a functional one and we trust it. If our golf swing is sound, we can repeat it easily with no conscious thought. Indeed, the swing will work better when we don't add extra thinking.

Perhaps the most important step in changing a golf swing, is to become aware of the thinking which causes us to move the club in the way we do. This thinking may not be obvious at first. It may well be happening at a subconscious level. If you can raise your awareness, you will begin to see those hidden patterns of thinking which cause your golf swing to happen in the way it does.

During an activity which is familiar to us, we aren't aware of what we are thinking moment to moment. There is an underlying flow of thought which we respond to almost automatically without realising we have a choice. This is particularly true in terms of movement, for example walking or driving a car. This may be the reason why a well established movement pattern is so hard to change. We just respond to thought on an instinctive level. The longer we have been doing something, the deeper in our subconscious this pattern of thought may be buried.

The problem comes when the movement pattern doesn't produce the results we want. We attempt to alter it in some way with conscious thought. An example is the urge to hit the ball as hard as possible, a temptation which many of us succumb to from time to time. We know from experience that this is a bad idea. It usually results in a poor shot. But from a low state of consciousness, we seem unable to stop ourselves from acting on the impulse to smash the living daylights out of the ball.

It is the same dip in awareness when we have a second piece of chocolate cake, even though we're not hungry, or that extra glass of wine even though we know we will regret it in the morning. We have the thought, and it must make sense to us from the level of consciousness we are in at that moment, because we act on it. From a higher level of consciousness, we would listen to our inner wisdom and would let the thought pass without action.

If we pay attention to the 'smash it' thought, and start to wind ourselves up both mentally and physically for a big swing at the ball, we will probably get an uneasy feeling. This our early warning system reminding us that our consciousness is low and we aren't seeing things clearly. Sometimes we misinterpret this feeling as excitement or anticipation, or it gets lost in the general levels of anxiety we mat be feeling at that point.

We can't control what thoughts come into our mind at a particular moment. Our level of consciousness is the only filter stopping us acting on the irrational, the dumb and the damaging. The moment we realise we are the one thinking the thought, our consciousness is raised to a level where we realise we have a choice whether to act or not. If we are below that crucial threshold of awareness, any thought can look like a good idea at the time.

The biggest factor in whether golfers make good or bad decisions on the golf course has little to do with course management skills or intelligence. It has every-thing to do with awareness of their levels of consciousness.

When you are trying to make a change in your golf swing, your awareness of what you are thinking is critical. We are creatures of habit. Your golf swing is a physical habit which developed over a period of time. When you play your best golf you don't think about it much. At some point however, when you were learning, you did think about it. You probably thought about it a great deal. The thoughts you had at that time resulted in the movement pattern you developed and practised and probably still have today.

Swing Archaeology.

Your golf swing is a living record of some thinking you did perhaps many years ago. Unless you get some fresh thinking, this movement pattern is not going to change. This is why the first step to changing your swing, is to get a good awareness and a good feel for what you currently do, in order to be able to uncover the thinking that initiates it. Only then will you be able to change it.

There are two common swing characteristics which golfers struggle to change. The first is an over the top, out to in swing path, the classic slicers move. The second is a weak flip through impact. The left wrist extends early in an attempt to increase loft on the club face and holds it open to compensate for the out to in path. No golfer wants to do either of these things in their swing, but many of them do. My question is why?

At one point in time, probably when they were learning to play, both of these movements felt like the correct thing to do. They made sense in terms of what the golfer thought they wanted to achieve at that moment. When we ask what the golfer might have been thinking in order to make a move like this, we can begin to understand why it made sense.

The steep, over the top swing has its origins in the first intention we have as golfers. We want to hit the ball. The ball is on the ground, so we swing the club up in the air with our arms to give it some momentum, then we swing it down to hit the ball. This movement becomes natural and instinctive the more we practice it. The club is swung up, and it is swung down. The ball is the only target of the movement.

We aren't really that bothered about where the shot goes. The priority is to make contact with the ball. A well meaning friend or instructor may have advised us to hit down on the ball. We practice with this thought in mind, until the movement becomes a habit. It might become exaggerated later on as we try to hit the ball further. I'll come back to that in a minute.

If the first thought in the mind of a new golfer is 'I want to hit the ball', the second intention is usually 'I want to hit the ball in the air'. The weak, flippy release that many golfers employ seems to be the result of this thought. They don't generate sufficient clubhead speed to launch the ball properly with backspin, so they add loft to the club face in an attempt to get it in the air and hit it a bit further.

They hit a few hundred golf balls with these two thoughts and the results are pleasing. They are now making regular contact, and the ball does indeed go in the air. They repeat this pattern of thinking. 'Swing the club down at the ball, lean the shaft back to make it go up'. This leads to an ingrained pattern of movement. This becomes their golf swing.

As they get more competent, their thinking about what they are doing retreats into the background. New thinking flows in over the old. Their intentions become subconscious. It still happens, but the golfer is much less aware of it. When a thought slides below our current level of consciousness, we still think it. It hasn't gone away. We just aren't aware that we think it. We only see the results of the thought in how we feel or what we do. The thought becomes 'The Missing Link' as Syd Banks describes.

When we first learn to drive a car the combination of movements to work the brake, clutch, gear shift, steering while watching the road and looking in the mirrors is very much at the forefront of our thinking. It can seem overwhelming. There is so much to think about. The movements become more automatic as we become more competent and get the hours of practice in. They require much less in the way of conscious thought.

We are able to think about other things as we drive along, like having a conversation or listening to the radio. The thought that we need to change gear or turn the steering wheel still happens, but unless we deliberately make the effort to tune into it, it happens at a level of thinking we are barely aware of.

At some point in our golfing lives our intentions start to change, as is the nature of thought. Inspired by playing with better golfers or watching the professionals play on television, our ambitions grow. Our first desire when we were learning was to hit the ball. Next we wanted to hit the ball in the air.

Now we can do this regularly, just making contact and getting it in the air doesn't seem quite so much fun. We see other golfers hitting it much further, and with a draw. Our weak slice begins to seem very unsatisfactory. We begin to realise that the over the top, out to in path we are swinging the club on is less than optimal. It's hard to hit the ball straight, and it doesn't go very far.

We have now been playing for a while, and we know a little bit about the golf swing. We start to think about what we should be doing to fix our slice. We read a few magazines, or take a lesson or two. We understand intellectually that the path of the swing needs to go to the right of the target, and the clubface needs to point left of that path. Unfortunately, our thinking at a deeper level is still repeating 'Swing the club down at the ball, lean the shaft back to make it go up'.

This leads to a great deal of confusion, and lots of thinking. We think we are doing one thing, but our body wants to do something different. The ball is flying all over the place. Frustration sets in. Thinking obstructs awareness, and our consciousness dips.

While all this thinking is happening, we can't get to a level of consciousness where we address the subconscious instincts and patterns of thought we have laid down previously. The underlying desire to 'swing the club down at the ball' is still there. We don't realise that the intended target for our swing needs to change, from being the little white ball on the ground between our feet, to being the green or fairway out there in the distance.

If we try to hit the ball further by just adding power to the over the top, out to in movement, things start to get even worse. The main sources of clubhead speed in a golf swing are rotation of the body, and rotation of the forearms. Think of the movement a baseball player makes when swinging at the ball. This natural swinging, throwing movement is powerful and efficient.

However, it needs to be directed properly, and it needs to be well timed, with speed being added as late in the downswing as possible. If this power move is directed at the ball on the ground, rather than at a distant target, the result is the golfer spinning his body faster and earlier from the top, causing the club to get even further away from the body as he starts down.

The over the top move will become more and more habitual unless the underlying thinking changes to 'swing the club to the target out in front and let the ball get in the way' instead of 'hit down on the ball and hit it up in the air'. The frustrations felt by the golfer will increase, levels of consciousness will descend and enjoyment of the game will be elusive.

> *'Thought always comes before behaviour (golf swing).*
> *You can't change a behaviour unless you change the*
> *thinking which is causing that behaviour.'*
>
> —*Garret Kramer.*

Once the golfer has the insight that their true intention is 'hit the ball,' they start to understand where the over the top movement comes from and can change it. Improvements come much easier and faster than people realise is possible. Your swing will change very quickly once the intention behind it doesn't make sense to you any more.

I have shared this with a couple of my students recently. Their swing path changed when they stopped seeing the ball as the target, swung the club to a target ten yards right of the flag stick, and just let the ball get in the way.

The changes in swing path were significant. From eight degrees out to in, to four or five degrees in to out. Awareness of the thought pattern that causes a movement, and changing it for a more appropriate intention has a dramatic effect. Thinking changes and so does the resulting pattern of behaviour the moment 'swing down at the ball' doesn't make sense any more.

As with so many aspects of human behaviour, the way we learn movement is perfectly adapted to work in our favour once we understand it. If you learn a functional movement pattern from the start, this swing becomes instinctive. The thinking that creates the movement becomes less conscious, and you can repeat the swing without thinking about it too hard. Once you have a pattern of functional thinking and functional movement, all you need to do is stay out of the way and let your instincts get on with it. Conscious thought at this point will make performance worse, not better.

Unfortunately, many golfers never get to that point of instinctive competence. They get caught up in a never ending cycle of fixing their golf swing. They never address the subconscious thinking behind what they do now. They never become aware of why they swing the way they do. They can't really feel their golf swing, so they never uncover the hidden thinking which causes them to move inefficiently.

I use the analogy of building a house. When you are in the construction phase, you make a mess. Rubbish gets everywhere, tiles and half bricks and bits of timber are strewn around. Mud, plaster and cement cover the floor.

When the work finishes you hire a skip to get rid of all the rubbish. You give the house a good clean before you move into it. You don't keep all the stuff we don't need lying around cluttering up the place. Doing so would make living in the house difficult and uncomfortable.

Your thought pattern when learning to swing is useful during the process, but not once it is established. If golf swings were houses, most of us would never move into them. They'd be full of rubbish. We are always rebuilding, fixing, renovating our golf swings. Yet we never seem to ask the simple question: Why do I swing the club like this?

Thought is the most wonderful, creative force. Thoughts help us learn and create functional golf swings. Once we have a swing that works we can get rid of a lot of the thoughts that helped create it. This de-cluttering, this removal of all the mental rubbish, is essential if we are to perform to our potential. If we don't understand that thoughts are meant to come and go, we might think we need to hang onto them in order to swing.

Most of us remember how mentally taxing it was learning to drive a car. Now we drive miles and miles every day as if it was second nature. Yet many of us try to play golf as if we are still learner drivers, by trying to control the swing with our intellectual thinking.

The Myth That Practice Makes Perfect.

It is accepted as fact that it takes a certain number of hours, or a certain number of repetitions to change, then ingrain a movement. In his book 'Outliers' author Malcolm Gladwell uses a number of examples to make the claim that the key to achieving world class expertise in any skill, is to a large extent, a matter of practicing the skill for a total of around 10,000 hours.

Despite the fact that most of Gladwell's evidence is circumstantial, this idea has been quoted so many times by various experts with reference to golf and other sports, that it has become an unquestioned law. Child prodigies such as Rory McIllroy, Tiger Woods and Phil Mickelson, who had golf clubs placed in their hands at a very early age, and then hit golf balls relentlessly for the next twenty years, are held up as proof of the adage that 'practice makes perfect'.

The idea looks like common sense. After all, if you do something every day, you usually get better at it. We often hear, 'the more you put in, the more you get out'. Unfortunately as Gladwell himself states in a later interview, there are other, more important factors that are a bigger determinant of success in a sporting context. He says,

'There is a lot of confusion about the 10,000 hours rule that I talk about in Outliers. It doesn't apply to sports. And practice isn't a SUFFICIENT condition for success. I could play chess for 100 years and I'll never be a grandmaster. The point is simply that natural ability requires a huge investment of time in order to be made manifest. Unfortunately, sometimes complex ideas get oversimplified in translation.'

—*Article by Drake Baer for www.BusinessInsider.com.*

I bought into this idea of work being equal to success despite building a file of evidence to the contrary. I've certainly clocked up 10,000 plus hours grinding away on the practice ground over thirty years of playing the game. I'm a good golfer. I shoot under par on a regular basis. But I wouldn't back myself with a lot of my own money against Jordan Spieth or Hideki Matsuyama, neither of whom were born when I first got my handicap down to scratch.

So, if 'putting in the hours' isn't the most significant factor in improving, what is? The answer lies more in our state of mind when we are doing what we do than just in the time we spend doing it. Improvement is a function of your level of consciousness when you are practising, rather than a matter of the hours you put in.

When your mind is clear and open, rather than regurgitating stale thinking, it is capable of offering insights. Insights are fresh, new thoughts which can enhance your performance in matter of minutes, rather than hours or days.

If you practice for ten minutes in a high state of consciousness, there's a very good chance you'll have an idea or an insight which will move you forward.

In his book 'How I Play Golf', Tiger Woods says,

'Never judge your practice sessions on how long you practiced or how many balls you hit. Some of my best practice sessions have lasted all of twenty minutes.'

Seven time European Order of Merit winner Colin Montgomerie was famous for his warm up before a tournament round. It usually consisted of a dozen balls on the range and a bacon sandwich in the caddy hut.

If you practice for 10,000 hours in a low mind-set, you'll end up frustrated, with blisters on your hands and your swing faults grooved. When I was playing full time I'd head to the range in a foul mood after a bad round to beat balls and swap hard luck stories with other grumpy and frustrated players.

Very rarely did these sessions result in significant improvements. I see so many golfers who practice hard, put in the time, but don't improve because they have a misunderstanding about how learning and improving actually works.

An insight which changes something significant in your golf can occur at any moment. We've all had the experience where 'something just clicked'. One minute the swing is awkward and ineffective. For some reason, our thinking changes, a different mental picture emerges, the feel is different. The next swing is effortless and the ball starts coming out of the middle of the clubface. Our consciousness went up, the thought pattern changed and as a result, so did the way we moved the golf club.

So does this mean we shouldn't practice, that we should just sit around and wait for inspiration to show up? Or that we should quit and go and do something else when the going gets difficult? Maybe, but probably not. Staying in the game', as Garret puts it, gives you the chance of being in a productive environment when your mind does clear and an insight occurs.

The mind is designed to self correct and clear naturally. Your awareness rises and previously unseen possibilities open up. This can happen at any time. If you are on the practice range when it happens, you can put your insight into action while it is fresh.

As Michael Neill says,

'If you want to catch a bus but you don't know what time it will arrive, your best course of action is probably to hang out at the bus stop.'

Stay in the game, or on the practice ground. Just be aware when you are starting to grind or force it. Putting in the time and effort to something you enjoy is one of the most pleasant ways to spend your non working hours. Approaching any activity with a high state of mind, or at least not with a low one, is the best way to make that time as enjoyable and productive as possible.

CHAPTER 9

How Do I Apply This?

'I still had nine holes to play, and I had the best player in the world tracking me down. He'd won Augusta two months before; he was the hot favourite.

No psychologist told me to do this – it came from the heavens – but every time there was a roar for Tiger, I imagined it was for me. In my mind I was saying, 'Thanks, thanks very much, thank you!'

'You have a choice of thoughts,' the once-and-always U.S. Open champion says, his gaze wandering off to the horizon, to the sea.

'It all depends on how you look at things.'

—Michael Campbell. 2005 US Open Champion. Interviewed by John Garrity for Golf.com

I'M HOPING BY NOW THAT YOU have a clearer understanding of the relationship between your thoughts and feelings, the importance of your levels of consciousness and awareness, and the benefits of trusting insights from your inner wisdom, rather than your intellect.

Thought is the creative principle, the tool we use to create our perception of reality. Thought on its own is powerless. It's what we do with thought, which of our thoughts we choose to bring to form that determines how our world looks to us and how we feel as a result.

Consciousness is the awareness principle. The way we experience life is through our ability to be aware of our thoughts. Without consciousness, thought would be irrelevant.

Mind is the spiritual intelligence behind our lives It's the space within us before thought. It's our soul, our inner wisdom. We play to our potential when we are feeling the connection to this place within. Life seems to flow with ease and fluency. We trust that we will be okay, that things happen for a reason, we are less attached to outcomes.

Life feels like a grind when our heads are filled with thought, and we lose our connection to wisdom, the still, quiet place within us, beyond form, beyond thought.

At this point in the book you might be thinking to yourself:

'I've got a sense of what you're trying to convey. I can see how misunderstanding the relationship between thought and feeling affects my state of mind. I can see how golf might change for me when I understand these principles more clearly. So what do I do now? How do I apply what I've learnt? What do I need to work on?'

As golfers, we're used to instructions, stuff to work on, step-by-step plans. What I'm suggesting is different, because there isn't anything you need to do. You already have what you're looking for. Just be aware that you're the thinker. Look towards your inner wisdom more than your intellect. Get on with living your life and playing your golf.

A common response is 'It can't be that simple'. The simple reply is, 'Why not?'

You might feel uneasy from time to time when you get caught up in the flow of thought, but you will start to read the signals more quickly. The best way to deepen your understanding of the three principles is to see how they play out in real life, in your own experience and in the people around you.

Notice changes in your feelings. Be aware when you get caught up in thought. An early lesson for me was looking back at a situation and realising I handled it differently than I normally would have. I didn't know why or how at the time.

The Human Operating System.

You can think of the principles I have described in the previous chapters as the operating system for the human mind. The computer I'm writing this book on came off the production line at the factory without any programs installed. A piece of software called the operating system was loaded onto the hard drive. This is the program that allows all the other software to work.

Up to this point I have tried to explain how the operating system functions. I haven't tried to tell you which programs you should run on the computer, or what sort of work or games you should use it for. I haven't told you what to do or to change what you believe.

This point is crucial. No one else has better answers for your life than you do. Be wary of anyone who tells you what to think, what to do, how you should feel or how to behave. That's why I, nor anyone else, can tell you how to apply what you have learnt so far.

If You Know it, You Don't Need to Apply It.

If you find yourself needing to apply what you have learned, it's because you have lost the feeling this book is pointing to. Please don't be discouraged. It's common to lose sight of how thought affects how we feel. If you are a goal-oriented person who likes the feeling of making things happen and ticking off a to do list, the lack of a plan might be disconcerting.

If these feelings are bother you, please go back and re-read chapters four through to seven again to remind yourself where they are coming from. Repetition is helpful when you first start to see this understanding. It's easy to miss the fact we are thinking. Insecure feelings are usually the first sign.

Thinking consciously about swinging a golf club is unnatural, just as thinking about other everyday movements is unnatural. I don't think about how to walk when I'm on the golf course. I walk. I don't think about technique when riding my bike. I just ride. When I get in my car, I drive. I don't run through a step by step plan in my head as I did when I was learning.

The state of mind when I play well is a sense that I don't have to do anything to play well or enjoy my golf. I can just go play.

When you have an embodied understanding of a principle, an activity, a capability, it's what you do naturally. You don't need to think about how to do it. You just get on with it.

This is a good way to determine if you have truly learnt something you want to bring to your game. If you have to think about how to do it, or apply a technique in order to execute it, you don't know it yet. When you've mastered a particular movement or skill, it becomes part of what you do instinctively, without conscious thought about how.

What is Gravity?

Having lived in gravity my whole life, I am an expert on living with its effects. I have a deep, embodied under-standing of the implications of dropping something, or losing my balance. As I write this chapter, scientists at L.I.G.O have just confirmed the existence of gravitational waves, proving what Einstein proposed in his theory of relativity one hundred years ago. I only have a sketchy understanding of the scientific theory, but I am familiar with the effects of gravity.

We know gravity is essential to our existence. Golf doesn't work very well as a game without it. However, we don't spend much time thinking about how it works, or how to apply techniques for dealing with it. We just get on with living life in its effects.

Occasionally, the effects of gravity might cause a problem. Somehow you lose your awareness or thoughts distract you. Maybe you knock something off a table, or drop a plate. Perhaps you lose your balance and trip or fall. Rather than devising a strategy to prevent it happening again, you deal with it and just get on with life. Your subconscious makes a little note to be more aware in similar situations. You learn from it and carry on.

Trying to apply a strategy to cope with your feelings or emotions is like trying to apply a strategy to cope with gravity. Feelings and emotions are just part of the human experience, the same way living in gravity is part of the human experience. Feelings arising from your thinking is a psychological fact just as gravity is a physical fact.

The more you see this dynamic in action, you learn to trust your feelings as a kind of emotional balance indicator. Anxious or insecure feelings are a little warning your thinking is ramping up. The moment you notice this, you will self-correct back towards balance. There is nothing to apply here. No technique or strategy required. Simply trust that the system works.

I find it helps if I remind myself to look in this direction – inside rather than outside. I like to read and listen to podcasts and audiobooks by Syd Banks, Garret Kramer, Jamie Smart, Elsie Spittle, Michael Neill and others. If possible, talk to someone who has been around this understanding a while and ask questions. You can find my contact details at the back of the book.

Everyone has a different story, different experiences, a slightly different way of explaining how the Principles look to them. The best way is just to live your life, and keep looking inwards at your state of mind rather than outwards at your situation or circumstances.

How Will I know When I Understand It?

The answer is simple. You'll feel less stressed, more peaceful more often and for longer. You might notice your thinking, but won't get upset by it. You won't struggle. You'll be more resilient. Doing nothing will seem like a better option than doing something. Stuff that used to bother you will just pass you by. Drama will seem like it happens in the background, or happens to other people while you rise above it. Most of the time you will only notice that the drama passed you by with hindsight.

No one on earth sees that they are thinking 100% of the time. The way the special effects department works is so seamless, that even people who have a deep understanding of how their mind works get fooled by it on occasions.

People like Garret, and Jamie, even those who knew Syd Banks and learned directly from him, George Pransky, Keith Blevens, Dicken Bettinger and Elsie Spittle will all say that at certain points in their lives they get down, frustrated, annoyed or sad, because that's how the human mind works.

That's the nature of the human experience. We think therefore we feel. Our thoughts change, and so do our feelings. It has been that way for thousands of years, and will continue to be so. The richness of this experience comes from our ability to feel those emotions. You wouldn't know happiness if you had never been sad. You wouldn't know excitement if you had never felt bored. You wouldn't know peace and contentment in the same way if you had never felt stressed or anxious.

First Tee Nerves.

I don't know any golfer who doesn't get a buzz from walking onto the first tee to play a round that means something to them. Welcome to golf as experienced by a human being. For many people, this feeling is one of the reasons they play the game. They love the feeling of excitement and anticipation.

Unfortunately for others, that buzz can go beyond excitement. It develops into such an unpleasant, insecure feeling that it becomes difficult to execute a normal golf swing. Let's go back and have a look at what we know about the nature of thought to explain these feelings, and what we can do about them.

Our feelings come from our thinking in the moment, not from the situation, even though it looks that way. It's the first tee, there are people watching, it's the first shot of the day and you want to get off to a good start. None of those things are the cause of your insecure feelings. Your thinking is the cause of your insecure feelings. The moment you see that you are the one doing the thinking, your mind will start to clear. Your consciousness and awareness levels will rise, you will get curious about something and the swing can happen in that clear space.

First tee nerves, or any other sort of nervous feelings, are not telling you anything about the situation or circumstances. They are simply telling you to look inside, not outside, and to step up and hit the shot.

Why do Golf Shots go Wrong?

You're coming down the last few holes of a medal round

or tournament. You've got a good score going. Your thinking revs up, and you misinterpret your nervous feelings, attributing them to the 'pressure' of the situation. You make a bad swing on the wrong hole and the ball sails out of bounds. You dwell on that one shot afterwards and conclude you need to fix your swing to stop it happening again. I spent about fifteen years doing this, and watching other people do it.

Your swing was working fine for the majority of the round. You were playing well until your mind became cluttered. It would be helpful to look inside at your state of mind when you stood over the shot that went out of bounds rather than the mechanics of your golf swing.

An error in timing is the main reason golf shots go wrong. Timing is affected by tension. Feeling tense and anxious is the result of insecure, doubtful thinking. Blaming your golf swing and working to fix it is like taking the wrong exit off a roundabout, then taking your car apart and putting it back together to ensure you never take a wrong turn.

Looking for a technical solution to a thought created problem is one of the biggest traps golfers fall into. The golf instruction industry perpetuates this misunderstanding. Books, magazines and websites lure you into believing they have a solution for swings that don't hold up under pressure.

Always looking outside at technique, rather than inside at state of mind is what draws golfers into a never-ending cycle of swing fixes and technical changes. No wonder so many golfers get worse before they get better.

It doesn't have to be like this. It shouldn't be like this for you from now on.

Losing Confidence.

Struggling golfers tell me they've lost confidence, or that confidence comes and goes. They blame it on external events and circumstances like a bad round or their golf swing. As we now know, our feelings come from our thinking, not from situations or outside circumstances. Your confidence may disappear, but it hasn't gone anywhere. Layers of thinking just cover it up.

Thinking can make us feel nervous, anxious and uneasy, the opposite of confident. When thinking subsides and your mind clears, which it will do naturally, your skills and abilities are still there. Confidence will return, and it can do so in an instant. We hit a good shot, our thinking changes and confidence comes flooding back. It may look like the shot changed our feelings, but there was something in between.

Confidence is our natural state when thinking doesn't get in the way. You only have to see children playing and having fun, trying and failing, learning and succeeding, to see confidence is innate. It doesn't come from outside from skills we've acquired. It just seems that way. Confidence was there all along.

Most children have plenty of confidence whether or not they have experience of the activity or game they're playing. Their skill or technique isn't great when they start, but it doesn't dent their confidence. They always give their best effort to whatever they attempt.

Many people think confidence comes from being good at something, from having practised something over and over until that skill is mastered. However, even people who are extremely competent sometimes lose confidence. If skill and experience gives you confidence then surely anyone who's mastered the game would be confident all the time?

The reason you feel confident when you're playing well is because your mind is clear. You don't have much thinking going on about what might happen, or what you should or shouldn't be doing. You just look at the target and swing the club. Confidence is simply clarity of mind – the absence of uncertain, insecure thinking.

But What About My Goals?

I set many goals before I saw the nature of the Inside Out understanding. I had them all written down. I looked at them daily and had affirmations to go with them. I was going to get my tour card at age twenty seven, win my first tour event at thirty, be a Ryder Cup player at thirty five and win a couple of majors along the way. I wanted a big house in the country, a Range Rover, a Porsche GT3 and to spend a lot of time on Scotland's best salmon rivers.

Looking back, setting goals, reviewing them and affirming them every day took a lot of thinking and mental energy. That should have been a warning sign.

Some of these things may still happen, or maybe they won't. I know now I'm going to be okay whatever happens. This is a relatively new feeling for me. I wasn't okay with not achieving goals I had set for myself, which led to the unhappiness and anxiety I felt during my playing days. I was an expert at the 'I'll be Happy When' game. Not surprisingly, I struggled.

Goal setting is often touted as an essential element for success. I think if that were the case, many more people would be successful. Most people set goals. In my experience few of those goals are achieved. Every season, hundreds of golfers set a goal of winning a European Tour or PGA Tour card. There are only a limited number of cards available each autumn. That's a lot of golfers for whom goal setting didn't work.

Now that I know where my feelings come from, no wonder I was struggling professionally and personally. In its simplest form, a goal is just a thought about getting somewhere or achieving something. This thought gets repeated over and over and over again. The operating system gets blocked and jammed up when we get stuck on a thought, whether it is a goal or any other type of thinking.

Thought is meant to flow, to change and adjust. When old, stale thinking hangs around we become too focussed and our perceptual field closes in. We miss opportunities for learning and growth that, ironically, might help us develop and move forward in the long term because we are fixated on short term results, on ticking goals off lists.

I love to hear people talk about aspirations, hopes and dreams rather than specific goals. It's helpful to set a general direction of travel. Feelings of purpose and motivation, the desire to train hard, practice diligently and persevere often come from having a vision about becoming the best golfer we can be.

Visions of future success can inspire us, but now we know where our feelings come from, it can be helpful to ask why we want to be successful in a particular endeavour. The illusion that attaining titles, trophies, money and 'security' will make us happy is one we can now see through. Numerous major winners admit asking themselves the same question after reaching the highest level in the game; 'Now what?'

It might help you to ask how you feel when you think about your own golf. Do you feel more inspired by playing your best golf in an important situation or about lifting a trophy? Do you care about what other people will think of your success, feel excited or pride at telling people about your single figure handicap, or look forward to the security banking the winner's cheque would give you?

None of these thoughts or feelings are wrong and everyone will have them at some point. But they don't come from the events or circumstances, or from the fact you maybe set them as goals. They come from what you think.

What if today's goal was to get less caught up in your thinking than yesterday? More awareness and higher levels of consciousness than yesterday? To trust your inner wisdom, to look towards the unknown rather than what you know? What if the only person you wanted to be better than was the person you were yesterday? How would that feel? What would that mean for your golf?

Live your life and play your golf full out and fearlessly. Doing something well for its own sake, rather than for what you think it can get you is one of the most satisfying, fulfilling feelings we can experience. You may or may not get to the places in your dreams. Your dreams may well change. Some days you will take two steps back and one step forward, but the goal for the next day remains the same. Just keep getting better. Keep moving along the path and see where it takes you. I think you'll find this leads to less thinking and judging, to happier feelings and, in the long term, more satisfaction with whatever you achieve in this world.

But What If I Don't Know?

Our thoughts generally consist of what we already know. We tend to churn them over and over. We run the same thought patterns. These thought patterns lead to moods or patterns of feeling, which lead to habits or patterns of physical behaviour. The lower our state of consciousness, the more real this thinking looks and the less we realise we have choice about believing it.

An insight is some fresh thinking, something you didn't know, something you weren't seeing, weren't aware of. Change can be found in what you don't know, but only rarely in what you already know. Thinking 'I know that', caused me a lot of trouble during my younger days.

Often we think we really know something, when in fact we have an intellectual overview, a conceptual understanding rather than a deep, embodied one. Some big insights came to me when I first started to see that my feelings come from my thinking. Life definitely changed for the better.

However, my thinking still looked real in certain situations. I'd get insecure and anxious, even though I had started to have some insights into why I was feeling insecure and anxious. This happened mainly on the golf course.

Whenever I felt nervous, I would tell myself: 'It's OK, you know it's just your thinking making you feel like this.' But the insecure feelings would remain. My newly discovered 'cure for anxiety' clearly wasn't helping me and I'd get more annoyed and frustrated. As my understanding deepened, I realised there's a difference between thinking 'I have a technique to cope with this', and allowing my feelings to settle instinctively.

My anxious feelings would have subsided if I had seen the story I was making up about a situation. What I did was make up another story about having a technique overcome my negative feelings. All techniques just lead to more mental clutter. So thinking 'I know it's my thinking' had the opposite effect to the one I was hoping for.

Your feelings are a fool-proof indicator of what's going on inside. If you don't feel good, it can only be one thing. You're seeing your thinking as real, rather than seeing yourself as the thinker.

I was at a training day with Jamie Smart. I explained how I was feeling. I told him that even though I understood my thoughts were made up, I was still feeling anxious. He asked a simple question that filled a big gap in my understanding. The conversation happened in front of a classroom of other people. I began to feel a bit agitated and insecure, wondering what they were thinking about me.

Jamie thought for a moment and then asked:

"Sam, what if you didn't know? What if at that moment you just accepted that you didn't know it was your thinking? How would that feel?"

I paused, and it slowly dawned on me that not knowing was actually okay. In fact, it was more than okay. I felt some unease drop away, felt my mind clear. My normal thinking pattern was to have all the possible answers to possible questions in my head. Jamie's question made me realise that this approach left no room for insight, for my inner wisdom to come up with fresh thought.

The moment you admit you don't have all the answers, the connection to wisdom opens up. Solutions you didn't even know were possible become available.

'An expert is a man who has made all the mistakes which can be made in a narrow field.'

—Niels Bohr

That session was a breakthrough for me. As a coach, someone who is expected to have all the answers, I was making up a story about needing to know, needing to have everything figured out, needing to be the 'expert'.

I played in a local tournament the following week. I played okay, shooting one-under-par to finish fourth.

The real satisfaction came from the way I felt on the golf course. I felt very calm and relaxed for most of the round. I got off to a good start. I began to sense that my thinking was trying to take me down the route of needing to play well,' of needing to hit a good shots and good putts. My usual anxious feelings started to return.

Then I remembered what Jamie said. I accepted I was a bit lost in my thinking and I didn't know what to do about it. I simply hit the next shot. I felt my mind quieten and my feelings settle as they had done at the training. My swing felt looser and I hit some really nice shots. It felt very different to telling myself that it was my thinking and willing myself to relax.

The Expectations Game.

A friend of mine played on the 2015 EuroPro Tour. He had a disappointing season. He's a really good player, but hadn't played as well as he'd hoped. Consequently, he began 2016 playing on the same tour rather than moving up to the European Challenge Tour as he'd anticipated.

We got together for a coffee and I asked him why he felt 2015 hadn't gone as planned?

'Not sure really,' he said. 'I just wasn't as clear as I wanted to be. I think I was too focused on results, rather than just playing and letting the results take care of themselves. I know I need to perform well to get to the next level, and I had a lot of thinking going on about that.'

I thought for a moment: 'Okay, I get that the score is

important. That's how you judge yourself and how other people judge you. But if I could give you a tablet that guaranteed you would shoot 68 every single time you went out to play, would you take it?'

He went quiet for a moment. 'I'm not sure,' he replied. 'Part of me would really like to say yes. It would mean I achieved a lot of my goals. The money would be nice. But I know I'd get bored with it after a while. I'd end up playing four times a year in the major championships. The challenge would have gone out of the game. I know I'd start thinking, why couldn't shoot 67, or 66 or 65?'

Most golfers understand this conversation. There would be little interest in playing if we knew what was going to happen after every swing. We want the element of the unknown. We love the game because it's challenging. We wouldn't be as keen if it was easy.

The relationship between thoughts and feelings offers an insight into why the game seems so much more enjoyable some days than others. We create our own version of reality with our thinking. We understand we can't really control what our thoughts are on a moment to moment basis. So when we play an important round, it's inevitable we're going to have thoughts about what would be an acceptable or ideal outcome.

This thinking is normal, natural and to a greater or lesser extent unavoidable. The creative nature of thought always throws up visions of how we would like the world to be. The problem starts when the world doesn't match that vision. Innocently, we forget we created the vision in the first place.

When we get attached to results or outcomes, we are always judging the gap between our expectations and the way things look like they might be going. We feel this thinking. Then we miss the fact we made up the goal, blame the situation and start trying to do something about it. Now we really are on a slippery slope.

When we understand that we alone create our vision of the world, we can just go and play. We don't need to manage or lower our expectations, or try not to think about them. We can think about whatever we like, knowing those thoughts can't affect our mood or behaviour unless we allow them to.

Decisions.

A powerful intellect is a useful tool. It's like having a powerful computer. Great if you know how to use it, useless if you don't. Most of us are familiar with the phrase 'garbage in, garbage out' in an IT context.

There is a difference between intellect and wisdom. Our intellect is like a clever filing system. It collects and collates information, and attaches values to that information and makes judgements on it. Wisdom is upstream of the intellect, so the intellect has no understanding of it.

We have all met people who are very clever, or who have a lot of knowledge, but seem to lack common sense. Their intellect seems to work against them. They have a habit of out-thinking themselves.

I became aware during my playing days that some of

the best golfers I played with weren't intelligent in the intellectual sense. However, they had great wisdom about their game and played with great common sense. They made good decisions and rarely over analysed situations as I often did. Most golf shots fall into two categories as far as decision making goes: the decision is simple or it doesn't matter. I know this sounds contradictory so let me explain.

I'm standing on a par-three hole. The flag is 160 yards away. There are no changes in elevation and no wind. I hit my eight-iron 155 yards, my seven-iron 165. My intellect tells me I have a problem. I'm between clubs. What should I do? Hit a soft seven, or swing hard with the eight? It looks like I'm going to have to change my normal swing to get the perfect result. The shot looks a bit more complicated than it did when I walked onto the tee as find myself between clubs. I might start to feel uneasy.

If I disregard my thinking and use my common sense, it doesn't actually matter what I hit. A good strike on the right line with either club leaves me five yards away, fifteen feet short or fifteen feet past the flag. According to PGA Tour stats package ShotLink, average distance from the pin from 160 yards is over twenty feet. I would be happy if I consistently hit it to fifteen feet from 160 yards. The anxious feelings weren't coming from the situation, they were coming from my thinking about the shot.

Over thinking around the green gets many golfers get into trouble. The simpler the shot, the more different ways there are of playing it. From a decent lie in the fringe you could play a putt, chip, pitch, lob or bunt it with a hybrid. We tie ourselves in knots thinking about which shot is correct and how to play it properly. This thinking causes anxiety and tension. When we mess it up we blame ourselves for picking the wrong shot. What made the shot more difficult was over thinking and our subsequent state of mind.

Common sense is telling you it doesn't matter. It's a simple shot. Any shot is the right one in this situation. The trap is over thinking it. Pick the shot you feel most comfortable with and play it. Go with your instincts rather than spend too much time listening to your intellect.

Competition.

Competing is important to many golfers. Winning is important. I love to play tournaments, to compete and sometimes to win. When we play to and beyond our potential, it encourages our fellow competitors to do the same. When the level of the game is raised, so is the potential and skills of the participants. Not playing flat out, giving less than our best effort questions the whole purpose of playing. By not playing in the spirit of the game we interfere with our connection to wisdom, our own spirit is enshrouded by thought.

I talked to Ian Poulter's father Terry about my idea for this book. I was surprised when he said he never let Ian or his other son Danny beat him when they played chipping or putting games as kids, or later when they played full rounds. Terry felt it was important for the boys to learn the true spirit of competition, to learn that all participants doing their best was more important than who won or who lost.

He wanted them to understand that they would be fine and life would go on whatever the result. This would allow them to play with freedom. Given their obvious talent for the game and how both loved to compete, he also knew it wouldn't be long before they'd be beating Dad fair and square.

The love of competition is strong motivation for many players. It isn't my place to tell someone that winning isn't important, or that it's okay to be a good loser, or to just play for fun. Everyone has different reasons for playing. Those reasons will change with the natural ebb and flow of thought.

Coaches and psychologists should be helping golfers understand where their experience is coming from, helping them see that they'll be fine win, lose or draw. A golfer's state of mind has nothing to do with the score or the match situation. The lesson is to understand that their thinking determines how they feel.

Simplicity.

'I would not give a fig for the simplicity on this side of complexity, but I would give my right arm for the simplicity on the other side.'

—Oliver Wendell Holmes.

The game of golf is simple when we are clear. At some point I had an innate understanding of how my thoughts were related to my feelings, but I lost sight of that fact and had to somehow rediscover it. Many of us follow the same path with our golf swings.

This awareness is in all of us from birth. Children don't worry that their feelings come and go. They can be upset to the point of hysteria one minute, then playing happily in the same situation five minutes later. They don't dwell on things. They don't really care how they feel, they just feel it, not worrying it might change in the next moment. They don't look for meaning in everything. They just get on with life. Many people look back with fondness on the ease and simplicity of early childhood, when we had no cares or worries. This is the simplicity on this side of complexity.

Life gets more confused as we grow older. Our parents and other adults innocently encourage us to associate our feelings in the moment with events in the outside world. If we are feeling happy and another child comes along and says something or does something and we start feeling upset or cross, it looks like they were the cause.

This is reinforced when an adult asks us what's wrong and then, with the best intentions, tries to change or fix the external circumstances to make us feel better. The role of our own thinking in the process is completely overlooked. Rather than portray us as victims, it would be far better if the above situation was used to explain how thoughts and feelings work on both sides, that the situation was in fact neutral.

The simplicity on the other side of complexity is

reached when we understand once again the role of our thoughts in explaining how we feel. Life becomes very simple when we see thought is the missing link between what happens to us and how we feel. We are no longer caught up in the complexity of the outside world.

We feel our thinking. That's it. Our thoughts will pass if we wait a little while. So will our feelings, just like when we were children.

It's often said golf is a simple game made complicated by people. I agree. I hope from these examples you can see how the relationship between thought and feeling makes the game simple again. This understanding allows us to ignore some of the myths, psychobabble and contradictions that surround the game, often propagated by people who really should know better.

The more we look towards simplicity, the easier it becomes to play as we did when we were young, full out and fearless. When we play the game for the sheer love of it, the better our performance and the more we will enjoy the game, whatever our results.

I'm aware of the irony of a 50,000 word book promoting the message of simplicity. As you look inwards, rather than outside, you'll see that the message is the same, but that there are any number of ways of saying it. Repetition can help. Keep looking inside. As your understanding deepens you'll find what most of us find, that the three principles of Mind, Consciousness and Thought, are actually one and the same thing. I think I'll save that insight for the next book.

CONCLUSION

'Point yourself in the right direction, then do nothing'.

—Syd Banks.

FOLLOWING DIVERSIONS INTO PHYSICS, PHILOSOPHY, RELIGION and the nature of the universe, we are at the end of our meandering journey. Thank you for staying with it.

I know some of you might have been thinking: 'Why is this relevant?'

Golf is a simple game. I just want to get better at hitting a ball with a stick. Why do I need all this other stuff?' The answer is simple: you don't.

If you have the clarity, resilience and mental fortitude to resist the short cuts and strategies your thinking will tempt you with, then please just play on. Keep it simple. Just play your game.

However, only a minority of golfers keep the game simple. Most of us are curious, which is a double edged sword. Most of get seduced. We think. We get pulled from the path of simplicity, of truth, and off into the world of form, technique, equipment changes, statistics, biomechanics and ballistics. I'm not saying these fields don't have something to offer. The information you find might improve your game by an extra five or ten percent, but rarely offers the transformation many of us are seeking.

Hopefully this book will help you to pause and reflect, will encourage you to look inwards rather than outwards. I hope it will reassure you that answers won't be found in a golf magazine, instruction book, trackman numbers, from a new golf coach or on televised golf.

Science doesn't have the answers, psychologists don't have the answers, religion doesn't have the answers and equipment manufacturers don't have the answers. The answers will be found in one place and one place only. They are inside you, within your own consciousness.

You are infinitely more capable, powerful and mentally resilient than you realise. You have a permanent connection to an intelligence so deep you can't begin to comprehend what might be found there. You have the capacity to create your own reality, to jump around the space time continuum, bring ideas and insights from the best special effects department in the world into the world of form. We are creative, resourceful learning animals. It's one of the reasons our species has been so successful.

Learning will happen naturally if we get out of our own way and play golf with presence of mind, with awareness. We learn to move by moving, not by thinking about it. A child may fall over around one hundred times as it learns to walk.

Human beings have evolved to become the fastest, most efficient learners of new skills on the planet. We are natural learners from the minute we are born. Learning is an innate ability that never leaves us. It doesn't matter how old you are, how physically fit you are, what your IQ is or what your genes are. The opportunity to learn something new and useful is always there.

Just as we learn best when we are aware and our mind is clear, we perform most efficiently when we don't make a big deal or think too much about what we're doing. Driving a car, brushing our teeth, shaving, preparing food or climbing the stairs, we perform these complex, skilful tasks with ease. We make hundreds of highly coordinated, complex movements every day without stress, fuss, or drama.

These movements are nothing special. Hitting a ball with a golf club is no more difficult or complicated than any of these tasks. It's our thinking that hinders our natural ability to perform the golf swing to our potential. We make the game more difficult with our thoughts about it.

Now you know how our world is created via thought, you will understand when I say I'm aware these words are just my thoughts at a moment in time. I know I will see things differently on another day. As I said at the start of Chapter Two, my story isn't the truth, it's just how I remember it and think about it now.

My mother writes books for children. I'm lucky to have some good friends who have written books about golf, others who write about the Three Principles. They look back on their previous work, whatever the subject matter, with a mixture of resignation and wishful thinking. Resignation that the nature of setting down your thoughts on a page will inevitably lead to you looking back at it in a few weeks, months or years, and wish you had done it differently.

Words are all we have to try to convey a feeling, whether it's the golf swing or something deeper about what it means to be human. Inevitably, I won't get close to the true nature of what we're all pointing towards. Much better writers than I have tried and happily admit they've come up short.

But does that mean we shouldn't try? I think the understanding I point to in the preceding pages is much too important to remain hidden.

The Three Principles we have explored in the previous chapters are the insight of one man, Sydney Banks. His enlightenment experience in the autumn of 1973 will I believe in fifty or one hundred years, be seen as a turning point for human beings and for this planet. When we see the pain and misery, death and destruction that human behaviour wreaks on each other and the environment, it makes me wonder whether enough people will wake up before it's too late.

We know that Banks wasn't the first to see where our experience comes from. He wasn't the first to realise it's perfectly possible for us to live in peace and harmony with ourselves and with each other. Others have seen the individual elements of this understanding.

Greek philosopher Aristotle, centuries later William Shakespeare and recently physicist David Bohm saw the nature of thought and how human beings create their own separate realities through their thinking. Tim

Gallwey, Fred Shoemaker and many top performers point to elevated levels of consciousness as the catalyst for playing beyond our potential.

All the mainstream philosophies are pointing to what Albert Einstein describes as the *'cosmic religious feeling'*. The intelligence of the natural world, and the notion of a spiritual energy behind the creation of the universe has fascinated wise men throughout the ages.

As I related in Chapter Seven, one of the frustrating aspects of religion is that it makes it difficult to talk about subjects such as the origins of the universe, elevated states of consciousness, unconditional love, and the oneness of life, without people taking a position based on their thoughts about a book written hundreds of years ago.

Their beliefs, whether positive or negative, taint the discussion, and prevent people opening up and looking inside. You end up either with an argument about which group has the best signpost, or a flat rejection that the signpost could be pointing to anything worth seeing. The opportunity to explore what it means to be a human being and to experience these feelings that we all have is diminished.

Syd Banks' genius was in expressing how human beings bring the Three Principles of Mind, Consciousness and Thought together to create their experience of life. He described his insight in simple, non-theological terms. Based on his own experience he described how the Three Principles can change a person's whole perception of life without anything else in their circumstances being different.

He realised that if such an insight could take him from depression and insecurity to enlightenment and peace, then the same could happen for anyone.

Syd Banks wasn't highly educated. He wasn't an intellectual in the sense that Einstein was. However, he saw something afresh and his world was transformed. Despite this profound insight, he didn't promote himself as a leader or a guru. He didn't tell people what to think and how to behave. He did the opposite.

He warned people about the dangers of being a follower, of adopting someone else's thoughts and beliefs. He kept pointing us back inside, towards our own inner wisdom and common sense, towards the understanding and the peace of mind so many of us seek.

Understanding how life works, and finding peace of mind is the most important part of the Banks' story and of your own story. If what you believe, the philosophy which guides you through life, doesn't bring a tangible feeling of happiness, contentment and peace, then it's just information, a theory.

What's the point of believing that theory, of knowing it if it doesn't bring you peace?

I still find myself wondering from time to time how nobody else saw what Banks did, how nobody described it in the simple, straightforward way he did. Maybe someone did and I'm not aware of it. Greek philosopher Plotinus comes close, describing his three pillars as 'The One', 'the Intellect' and 'the Soul'.

Sometimes the obvious is hidden in plain sight. Maybe Banks' lack of formal education meant he wasn't afraid of speaking out. As with the child pointing out that the Emperor's new clothes are not actually clothes at all, maybe it takes a certain naivety to stand up and express something which seems so obvious.

We feel what we think about. Our reality is created via our thoughts. All of the unhappiness and damaging behaviour in the world can be brought back to this one fact: People do what they do because from their level of consciousness it makes sense to them in the moment.

Unhappy, stressful thoughts lead to anxious, insecure feelings which lead to errant, destructive behaviour. Hopeful, grateful, optimistic thoughts lead to feelings of peace, positivity, happiness and contentment.

So what does understanding the Three Principles mean for you as a golfer?

Golf is a simple game, which golfers overcomplicate and make difficult for themselves by thinking about it too much. They do too much Head Stuff.

Up until a couple of hundred years ago, psychology was the study of the mind and the soul. Unfortunately, talking about the soul was the jealously defended territory of religion. Psychology became the study of the brain and of behaviour. Modern psychology, including sports psychology, is still stuck in this outward looking rut. We just don't appreciate the simple way the mind really works. The brain doesn't need much studying once you understand the principles of Mind, Consciousness and Thought if all you are looking for is a good feeling when you play.

Syd always urged us to look towards simplicity, towards common sense. He rarely offered advice, always pointing people in the direction of their own inner wisdom. He would do the same for a golfer who asked him how they might improve their game, or how they might enjoy it more.

I think he might have said something like this;

You already have what you are looking for. You won't find it with intellectual thought. It's all about the feeling. Play your golf. Wait and listen for a good feeling.

Be grateful for the opportunity you have to play a beautiful game, in beautiful places, with like minded people. You golfers are very lucky people. Gratitude will give you the feeling you are looking for.

No one has better answers for your golf than you do. No one is wiser than you are. No one is tougher, more resilient, or mentally stronger than you are. We all have access to the same spiritual intelligence that wisdom and resilience comes from.

You'll know when you've got it. The feeling will tell you. You'll step up to the ball knowing there is nothing you need to do to hit a good shot.

Trust your inner wisdom. Look inwards beyond the content of your own thinking. There's a place inside where nothing is impossible.

Thanks Syd.

* * *

Thank you for reading my book!

If you enjoyed it, I'd be really grateful if you could spend a couple of minutes writing a short review at the place where you bought it.

If you'd like to get in touch, please use drop me an email or connect via Twitter and Facebook. Contact details are below.

I have written a short bonus chapter, which includes a couple of fresh insights I had after the book was completed. You can download it here www.samjarmangolf.com/3pog-bonus

Thanks again,
Sam.

www.samjarmangolf.com
sam@samjarmangolf.com
facebook.com/samjarmangolf
@samjarmangolf

About the author

Sam lives in Wavendon, Buckinghamshire, a short drive from Woburn Golf Club where he has been a member for the last 27 years. Away from the golf course he enjoys walking his dog Daisy, salmon fishing, skiing, playing cards, reading and writing.